P9-CNB-089

DOVER · THRIFT · EDITIONS

When I Was a Slave

Memoirs from the Slave Narrative Collection

EDITED BY

NORMAN R. YETMAN

DOVER PUBLICATIONS, INC.
Mineola, New York

DOVER THRIFT EDITIONS

GENERAL EDITOR: PAUL NEGRI
EDITOR OF THIS VOLUME: KATHY CASEY

Copyright

Introduction copyright © 2002 by Dover Publications, Inc.
All rights reserved under Pan American and International Copyright Conventions.

Published in Canada by General Publishing Company, Ltd., 895 Don Mills Road, 400-2 Park Centre, Toronto, Ontario M3C 1W3.

Published in the United Kingdom by David & Charles, Brunel House, Forde Close, Newton Abbot, Devon TQ12 4PU.

Bibliographical Note

This Dover edition, first published in 2002, is a republication of selected unabridged narratives from the Slave Narrative Collection developed from interviews recorded and transcribed by the Federal Writers' Project, 1936–38, some of which were published in *Voices From Slavery* (edited by Norman R. Yetman; first published in 1970 by Holt, Rinehart and Winston, Inc., New York; republished by Dover Publications in 2000). The Introduction by Norman R. Yetman was written for the 2002 edition.

Library of Congress Cataloging-in-Publication Data

When I was a slave : memoirs from the Slave Narrative Collection / edited by Norman R. Yetman.

    p. cm. – (Dover thrift editions)
    Narratives originally recorded by the Federal Writers' Project between 1936 and 1938 under the sponsorship of The Library of Congress and compiled as a manuscript collection under the title Slave narratives in 1941, subsequently referred to as the Slave Narrative Collection.
    ISBN 0-486-42070-1 (pbk.)
    1. Slaves—United States—Biography. 2. African Americans—Interviews. I. Yetman, Norman R., 1938– II. Federal Writers' Project. III. Slave narratives. IV. Series.

E444 .W5642002
305.5'67'09273—dc21

          2002019227

Manufactured in the United States of America
Dover Publications, Inc., 31 East 2nd Street, Mineola, N.Y. 11501

Acknowledgments

I am indebted to Raena Gardner, Catherine Heim, Sheri Johnson, Holly Krebs, Cara Lakin, Aaron Paden, and Terri Rockhold, who read a voluminous number of the narratives and assisted me in selecting those that we collectively felt were the most compelling and revealed most vividly the realities of slave life.

N.R.Y.

Introduction

The Great Depression of the 1930s was the most devastating economic crisis ever experienced in the United States. In response to massive unemployment throughout the entire country, the federal government under the administration of Franklin D. Roosevelt created a wide range of programs to achieve economic recovery. Among the most prominent of these New Deal programs was the Works Progress Administration (WPA), which was designed to put unemployed people to work using their skills on public-works projects such as building roads, dams, bridges, and swimming pools. However, because unemployment was so widespread and affected not only unskilled and blue-collar workers, the WPA included work projects for unemployed white-collar workers as well. These federally supported relief projects were implemented through the Federal Arts Project, an umbrella organization that included the Federal Art, Music, Theatre, and Writers' Projects, which were designed to assist unemployed artists, musicians, actors, and writers by providing them with employment that would utilize their skills. With its creation the federal government embarked upon an unprecedented program of support for artistic and cultural endeavors.

One of the most noteworthy and enduring achievements of the WPA was the Slave Narrative Collection, a group of autobiographical accounts of former slaves. Compiled in seventeen states during the years 1936–38, the Collection consists of more than two thousand interviews with former slaves. The interviews, most of them first-person accounts of slave life and the respondents' personal reactions to bondage, afforded aged ex-slaves an unparalleled opportunity to have recorded for posterity their personal accounts of slave life, to describe in their own words what it had felt like to be a slave in the United States.

The Slave Narrative Collection provides a unique and virtually unsurpassed collective portrait of a historical population. Indeed, historian David Brion Davis has argued that the voluminous number of documented slave testimonies available in the United States—the vast majority of which are interviews with former slaves by members of the Federal Writers' Project—"is indisputably unique among former slaveholding nations." In addition to the large number of personal accounts that it contains, the Collection is invaluable because of the great diversity of the slave experiences that were reported. The ex-slaves ranged in age from one year old to more than fifty at the time of emancipation in 1865. More than two-thirds were older than eighty when they were interviewed, more than seventy years after slavery was legally ended. Almost all had experienced slavery within the states of the Confederacy and still lived there. All major slave occupations were represented. Moreover, the size of the slave units on which respondents reported living varied considerably, from plantations with more than a thousand slaves to situations in which the informant was the only slave. The treatment these individuals reported ran the gamut from the most harsh, impersonal, and exploitative to living and working conditions that were intimate and benevolent. The WPA ex-slave interviews thus constitute an illuminating and invaluable source of data about Southern life before, during, and after the Civil War; about the institution of slavery; and, most important, about the reactions, responses, and perspectives of those who had been enslaved.

The national office of the Federal Writers' Project requested that copies of the interviews obtained by state and local Writers' Project workers be forwarded to Washington, D.C. The narratives then were organized into the nineteen-volume series that became known as the Slave Narrative Collection, which was deposited in the Rare Book Room of the Library of Congress. However, because materials found in the Rare Book Room can be examined only in the Library of Congress itself, the interviews were for many years relatively inaccessible to a broad readership. The existence of the Collection was first publicized in 1945 with the publication of B. A. Botkin's *Lay My Burden Down*, which is comprised of excerpts and selections from the Collection. While *Lay My Burden Down* vividly captures the flavor of the Collection's contents, only a handful of the more than two thousand interviews in the Collection were reprinted in their entirety. Responding to the need to make complete interviews more widely available, in 1970 I published *Voices From Slavery* (also published in a text edition under the title *Life Under the "Peculiar Institution"*), which contains 100 complete interviews. In 1972 and 1973 Greenwood Press published *The American Slave: A Composite Autobiography*, under the editorship of George Rawick. This sixteen-volume series included the entire Slave Narrative Collection, as well as two volumes of interviews conducted in the 1930s at Fisk University. The *American Slave* series was extended in 1977 and 1979, when Greenwood published an additional twenty-two volumes of interviews with former slaves, most of them collected as part of the Federal Writers' Project efforts but not included in the Slave Narrative Collection.

In 2000 Dover Publications reissued *Voices from Slavery*, which, in addition to the interviews with former slaves, contains essays describing the history of the Slave Narrative Collection and its impact on the scholarship about American slavery. The primary objective of *When I Was a Slave*, which includes some interviews previously published in *Lay My Burden Down* and *Voices From Slavery*, is to provide the reader with a concise introduction to the Slave Narrative Collection by reprinting some of the most detailed, compelling, and engrossing life histories in it. I have edited the narratives only slightly—primarily to improve readability and continuity. I have sought to achieve some uniformity of dialect spelling, but at no point have the metaphors or the patterns of speech themselves been changed. Because the primary goal of the project to interview former slaves was to gain information on their recollections of slave life and emancipation, I did omit occasional comments, usually very brief, about informants' living conditions when they were interviewed. Readers interested in viewing the entire Slave Narrative Collection are fortunate that the Library of Congress has recently made it available over the Internet at:

http://memory.loc.gov:8081/ammem/snhtml/snhome.html/

NORMAN R. YETMAN
The University of Kansas

Narrators

Mary Anderson
Mary Armstrong
Frank Bell
Boston Blackwell
W. L. Bost
Julia Brown
Anthony Dawson
Millie Evans
Mrs. M. S. Fayman
John Finnely
Delia Garlic
Robert Glenn
Andrew Goodman
Arnold Gragston
Mary Ella Grandberry
Sarah Gudger
Martin Jackson

Silas Jackson
Lewis Jenkins
Tines Kendricks
Fannie Moore
William Moore
Andrew Moss
Delicia Patterson
Mary Reynolds
Harriett Robinson
Tom Robinson
Robert Shepherd
Bill Simms
Ben Simpson
Gus Smith
Rosa Starke
Mingo White
Rose Williams

MARY ANDERSON

Interviewed near Raleigh, North Carolina
Interviewed by Pat Matthews
Age when interviewed: 86

MY NAME is Mary Anderson. I was born on a plantation near Franklinton, Wake County, North Carolina, May 10, 1851. I was a slave belonging to Sam Brodie, who owned the plantation at this place. My missus was Evaline. My father was Alfred Brodie and my mother was Bertha Brodie.

We had good food, plenty of warm homemade clothes, and comfortable houses. The slave houses were called the quarters, and the house where Marster lived was called the Great House. Our houses had two rooms each, and Marster's house had twelve rooms. Both the slave and white folks buildings were located in a large grove one mile square covered with oak and hickory-nut trees. Marster's house was exactly one mile from the main Louisburg Road and there was a wide avenue leading through the plantation and grove to Marster's house. The house fronted the avenue east and in going down the avenue from the main road you traveled directly west.

The plantation was very large and there were about two hundred acres of cleared land that was farmed each year. A pond was located on the place and in winter ice was gathered there for summer use and stored in an ice house which was built in the grove where the other buildings were. A large hole about ten feet deep was dug in the ground; the ice was put in that hole and covered. A large frame building was built over it. At the top of the earth there was an entrance door and steps leading down to the bottom of the hole. Other things besides ice were stored there. There was a still on the plantation and barrels of brandy were stored in the ice house, also pickles, preserves, and cider. Many of the things we used were made on the place. There was a grist mill, tannery, shoe shop, blacksmith shop, and looms for weaving cloth.

There were about one hundred and sixty-two slaves on the plantation. Every Sunday morning all the children had to be bathed, dressed, and their hair combed, and carried down to Marster's for breakfast. It was a rule that all the little colored children eat at the Great House every Sunday morning in order that Marster and Missus could watch them eat so they could know which ones were sickly and have them doctored.

Sunday was a great day on the plantation. Everybody got biscuits, Sundays. The slave women went down to Marster's for their Sunday allowance of flour. All the children ate breakfast at the Great House and Marster and Missus gave out fruit to all. The slaves looked forward to Sunday as they labored through the week. It was a great day. Slaves received good treatment from Marster and all his family.

The slave children all carried a mussel shell in their hands to eat with up to the Great House. The food was put on large trays and the children all gathered around and ate, dipping up their food with their mussel shells which they used for spoons. Those who refused to eat or those who were ailing in any way had to come back to the Great House for their meals and medicine until they were well.

Marster had a large apple orchard in the Tar River low grounds and up on higher ground and nearer the plantation house there was on one side of the road a large plum orchard and on the other side was an orchard of peaches, cherries, quinces, and grapes. We picked the quinces in August and used them for preserving. Marster and Missus believed in giving the slaves plenty of fruit, especially the children.

Marster had three children, one boy named Dallas, and two girls, Bettie and Carrie. He would not allow slave children to call his children "Marster" and "Missus" unless the slave said "Little Marster" or "Little Missus." He had four white overseers, but they were not allowed to whip a slave. If there was any whipping to be done he always said he would do it. He didn't believe in whipping, so when a slave got so bad he could not manage him, he sold him.

Marster didn't quarrel with anybody; Missus would not speak short to a slave, but both Marster and Missus taught slaves to be obedient in a nice quiet way. The slaves were taught to take their hats and bonnets off before going into the house, and to bow and say, "Good mornin' Marster Sam and Missus Evaline." Some of the little Negroes would go down to the Great House and ask them when it was going to rain, and when Marster or Missus walked in the grove the little Negroes would follow along after them like a gang of kiddies. Some of the slave children wanted to stay with them at the Great House all the time. They knew no better, of course, and seemed to love Marster and Missus as much as they did their own mother and father. Marster and Missus always used gentle means to get the children out of their way when they bothered them and the way the children loved and trusted them was a beautiful sight to see.

Patterrollers were not allowed on the place unless they came peacefully, and I never knew of them whipping any slaves on Marster's place. Slaves were carried off on two horse wagons to be sold. I have seen several loads leave. They were the unruly ones. Sometimes he would bring back slaves; once he brought back two boys and three girls from the slave market.

We were allowed to have prayer meetings in our homes and we also went to the white folks' church. But they would not teach any of us to read and write. Books and papers were forbidden. Marster's children and the slave children played together. I went around with the baby girl Carrie to other plantations visiting. She taught me how to talk low and how to act in company. My association with white folks and my training while I was a slave is why I talk like white folks.

The War was begun and there were stories of fights and freedom. The news went from plantation to plantation and while the slaves acted natural and some even more polite than usual, they prayed for freedom.

Then one day I heard something that sounded like thunder and Marster and Missus began to walk around and act queer. The grown slaves were whispering to each other. Sometimes they gathered in little gangs in the grove. Next day I heard it again, boom, boom, boom. I went and asked Missus, "Is it going to rain?" She said, "Mary, go to the ice house and bring me some pickles and preserves." I went and got them. She ate a little and gave me some. Then she said, "You run along and play."

In a day or two everybody on the plantation seemed to be disturbed and Marster and Missus were crying. Marster ordered all the slaves to come to the Great House at nine o'clock. Nobody was working and slaves were walking over the grove in every direction. At nine o'clock all the slaves gathered at the Great House and Marster and Missus came out on the porch and stood side by side. You could hear a pin drop everything was so quiet. Then Marster said, "Good morning," and Missus said, "Good morning, children." They were both crying. Then Marster said, "Men, women, and children, you are free. You are no longer my slaves. The Yankees will soon be here." Marster and Missus then went into the house; got two large arm chairs and put them on the porch facing the avenue and sat down side by side and remained there watching.

In about an hour there was one of the blackest clouds coming up the avenue from the main road. It was the Yankee soldiers. They finally filled the mile-long avenue reaching from Marster's house to the main Louisburg Road and spread out over the mile-square grove. The mounted men dismounted. The footmen stacked their shining guns and began to build fires and cook. They called the slaves, saying, "You are free."

Slaves were whooping and laughing and acting like they were crazy. Yankee soldiers were shaking hands with the Negroes and calling them Sam, Dinah, Sarah, and asking them questions. They busted the door to the smokehouse and got all the hams. They went to the icehouse and got several barrels of brandy: such a time! The Negroes and Yankees were cooking and eating together. The Yankees told them to come on and join them, they were free. Marster and Missus sat on the porch and they were so humble no Yankee bothered anything in the Great House.

The slaves were awfully excited. The Yankees stayed there, cooked, ate, drank, and played music until about night. Then a bugle began to blow and you never saw such getting on horses and lining up in your life. In a few minutes they began to march, leaving the grove which was soon silent as a graveyard. They took Marster's horses and cattle with them and joined the main army and camped just across Cypress Creek one and one-half miles from my marster's place on the Louisburg Road.

When they left the county, lot of the slaves went with them and soon there were none of Marster's slaves left. They wandered around for a year from place to place, fed and working most of the time at some other slave owner's plantation and getting more homesick every day.

The second year after the surrender our Marster and Missus got on their carriage and went and looked up all the Negroes they heard of who ever belonged to them. Some who went off with the Yankees were never heard from again. When Marster and Missus found any of theirs they would say, "Well, come on back home." My father and mother, two uncles and their families moved back. Also Lorenze Brodie and John Brodie and their families moved back. Several of the young men and women who once belonged to him came back. Some were so glad to get back they cried, 'cause fare had been mighty bad part of the time they were rambling around and they were hungry.

When they got back Marster would say, "Well, you have come back, have you?" And the Negroes would say, "Yes, Marster." Most all spoke of them as "Missus" and "Marster" as they did before the surrender, and getting back home was the greatest pleasure of all. We stayed with Marster and Missus and went to their church, the Maple Springs Baptist Church, until they died.

Since the surrender I married James Anderson. I had four children, one boy and three girls.

MARY ARMSTRONG

Interviewed at Houston, Texas
Interviewer not identified
Age when interviewed: 91

YOU ALL has to 'cuse me if I don't talk so good, 'cause I'se been feelin' poorly for a spell and I ain't so young no more. Law me, when I think back what I used to do, and now it's all I can do to hobble 'round a little. Why, Miss Olivia, my mistress, used to put a glass plumb full of water on my head and then have me waltz round the room, and I'd dance so smoothlike, I don't spill nary drop.

That was in St. Louis, where I'se born. You see my mama belong to Old William Cleveland and Old Polly Cleveland, and they was the meanest two white folks what ever live, cause they was always beatin' on their slaves. I know, cause Mama told me, and I hears about it other places, and besides, Old Polly, she was a Polly devil if there ever was one, and she whipped my little sister what was only nine months old, and just a baby, to death. She come and took the diaper offen my little sister and whipped till the blood just ran—just 'cause she cry like all babies do, and it kilt my sister. I never forgot that, but I got some even with that Old Polly devil and it's this-a-way.

You see, I'se 'bout ten year old and I belongs to Miss Olivia, what was that Old Polly's daughter, and one day Old Polly devil comes to where Miss Olivia lives after she marries, and tries to give me a lick out in the yard, and I picks up a rock about as big as half your fist and hits her right in the eye and busted the eyeball, and tells her that's for whippin' my baby sister to death. You could hear her holler for five miles, but Miss Olivia, when I tells her, says, "Well, I guess Mama has learnt her lesson at last." But that Old Polly was mean like her husband, Old Cleveland, till she die, and I hopes they is burnin' in torment now.

I don't 'member 'bout the start of things so much, 'cept what Miss Olivia and my mama, her name was Silvy, tells me. 'Course, it's powerful cold in winter times and the farm was lots different from down here. They calls 'em plantations down here, but up at St. Louis they was just called farms, and that's what they were 'cause we raises wheat and barley and rye and oats and corn and fruit.

The houses was builded with brick and heavy wood, too, 'cause it's cold up there, and we has to wear them warm clothes and they's wove on the place, and we works at it in the evenin's.

Old Cleveland takes a lot of his slaves what was in "custom" and brings 'em to Texas to sell. You know he wasn't 'sposed to do that, 'cause when you's in "custom," that's 'cause he borrowed money on you, and you's not 'sposed to leave the place till he paid up. 'Course, Old Cleveland just tells the one he owed the money to, you had run off, or squirmed out some way, he was that mean.

Mama say she was in one bunch and me in 'nother. Mama had been put before this with my papa, Sam Adams, but that makes no difference to Old Cleveland. He's so mean he never would sell the man and woman and chillen the same one. He'd sell the man here and the woman there and if they's chillen he'd sell them someplace else. Oh, old Satan in torment couldn't be no meaner than what he and Old Polly was to they slaves. He'd chain a nigger up to whip 'em and rub salt and pepper on him, like he said, "to season him up." And when he'd sell a slave, he'd grease their mouth all up to make it look like they'd been fed good and was strong and healthy.

Well, Mama say they hadn't no more'n got to Shreveport before some law man catch Old Cleveland and takes 'em all back to St. Louis. Then my little sister's born, the one Old Polly devil kilt, and I'se about four year old then.

Miss Olivia takes a likin' to me and though her papa and mamma so mean, she's kind to everyone, and they just love her. She marries to Mr. Will Adams what was a fine man, and has about five farms and five hundred slaves, and he buys me for her from Old Cleveland and pays him twenty-five hundred dollars, and gives him George Henry, a nigger, to boot. Lawsy, I'se sure happy to be with Miss Olivia and away from Old Cleveland and Old Polly, 'cause they kilt my little sister.

We lives in St. Louis on Chinqua Hill, and I'se house girl, and when the babies starts to come I nusses 'em and spins thread for clothes on the loom. I spins six cuts of thread a week, but I has plenty of time for myself and that's where I larns to dance so good. Law, I sure just crazy about dancin'. If I'se settin' eatin' my victuals and hears a fiddle play, I gets up and dances.

Mr. Will and Miss Olivia sure is good to me, and I never calls Mr. Will "Massa" neither, but when they's company I calls him Mr. Will and round the house by ourselves I calls them "Pappy" and "Mammy," 'cause they raises me up from the little girl. I hears Old Cleveland done took my mamma to Texas again but I couldn't do nothin', 'cause Miss

Olivia wouldn't have much truck with her folks. Once in a while Old Polly comes over, but Miss Olivia tells her not to touch me or the others. Old Polly tries to buy me back from Miss Olivia, and if they had they'd kilt me sure. But Miss Olivia say, "I'd wade in blood as deep as hell before I'd let you have Mary." That just the very words she told 'em.

Then I hears my papa is sold some place I don't know where. 'Course I didn't know him so well, just what mamma done told me, so that didn't worry me like Mamma being took so far away.

One day Mr. Will say, "Mary, you want to go to the river and see the boat race?" Law me, I never won't forget that. Where we live it ain't far to the Miss'sippi River and pretty soon here they comes, the *Natchez* and the *Eclipse*, with smoke and fire just pourin' out of they smoke-stacks. That old captain on the *Eclipse* starts puttin' in bacon meat in the boiler and the grease just comes out a-blazin' and it beat the *Natchez* to pieces.

I stays with Miss Olivia till '63 when Mr. Will set us all free. I was 'bout seventeen year old then or more. Away I goin' to find my mamma. Mr. Will fixes me up two papers, one 'bout a yard long and the other some smaller, but both has big gold seals what he says is the seal of the State of Missouri. He gives me money and buys my fare ticket to Texas and tells me they is still slave time down there and to put the papers in my bosom but to do whatever the white folks tells me, even if they wants to sell me. But he say, "Before you gets off the block, just pull out the papers, but just hold 'em up to let folks see and don't let 'em out of your hands, and when they sees them they has to let you alone."

Miss Olivia cry and carry on and say be careful of myself 'cause it sure is rough in Texas. She give me a big basket what had so much to eat in it I could hardly heft it and another with clothes in it. They puts me in the back end of the boat where the big old wheel what run the boat was and I goes to New Orleans and the captain puts me on another boat and I comes to Galveston, and that captain puts me on another boat and I comes up this here Buffalo Bayou to Houston.

I looks round Houston, but not long. It sure was a dumpy little place then and I gets the stagecoach to Austin. It takes us two days to get there and I thinks my back busted sure enough, it was such rough ridin'.

Then I has trouble sure. A man ask me where I goin' and says to come along and he takes me to a Mr. Charley Crosby. They takes me to the block what they sells slaves on. I gets right up like they tells me, 'cause I 'lects what Mr. Will done told me to do, and they starts biddin' on me. And when they cried off and this Mr. Crosby come up to get me, I just pulled out my papers and helt 'em up high and when he sees 'em he say, "Let me see them." But I says, "You just look at it up here." He squints up and say, "This gal am free and has papers." And tells me he a legislature man and takes me and lets me stay with his slaves. He is a good man.

He tells me there's a slave refugee camp in Wharton County but I didn't have no money left, but he pays me some for workin' and when the War's over I starts to hunt Mama again, and finds her in Wharton County near where Wharton is. Law me, talk about cryin' and singin' and cryin' some more, we sure done it. I stays with Mama till I gets married in 1871 to John Armstrong. And then we all comes to Houston.

I gets me a job nussin' for Dr. Rellaford and was all through the yellow fever epidemic. I 'lects in '75 people die just like sheep with the rots. I'se seen folks with the fever jump from their bed with death on 'em and grab other folks. The doctor saved lots of folks, white and black, 'cause he sweat it out of 'em. He mixed up hot water and vinegar and mustard and some else in it.

But, law me, so much is gone out of my mind, 'cause I'se ninety-one year old now and my mind just like my legs, just kinda hobble round a bit.

FRANK BELL

Interviewed at Madisonville, Texas
Interviewer not identified
Age when interviewed: 86[+]

I WAS owned by Johnson Bell and born in New Orleans, in Louisiana. Accordin' to the bill of sale, I'm eighty-six years old, and my master was a Frenchman and was real mean to me. He run a saloon and kept bad women. I don't know nothing about my folks, if I even had any, 'cept Mama. They done tell me she was a bad woman and a French Creole.

I worked round master's saloon, kept everything cleaned up after they'd have all night drinkin' parties, men and women. I earned nickels to tip off where to go, so's they could sow wild oats. I buried the nickels under rocks. If Master done cotch me with money, he'd take it and beat me nearly to death. All I had to eat was old stuff those people left, all scraps what was left.

One time some bad men come to Master's and gets in a shootin' scrape and they was two men kilt. I sure did run. But Master cotch me and make me take them men to the river and tie a weight on them, so they'd sink and the law wouldn't get him.

The clothes I wore was some Master's old ones. They always had holes in them. Master he stay drunk nearly all time and was mean to his slave. I'm the only one he had, and didn't cost him nothing. He have bill of sale made, 'cause the law say he done stole me when I'm small child. Master kept me in chains sometimes. He shot several men. I didn't have no quarters but stays round the place and throw old sack down and lay there and sleep. I'm afraid to run, 'cause Master say he'd hunt me and kill nigger.

When I'm about seventeen I marries a gal while Master on drunk spell. Master he run her off, and I slips off at night to see her, but he finds it out. He takes a big, long knife and cuts her head plumb off, and ties a great, heavy weight to her and makes me throw her in the river. Then he puts me in chains and every night he come give me a whippin' for a long time.

9

When war come, Master swear he not gwine fight, but the Yankees they captures New Orleans and throws Master in a pen and guards him. He gets a chance and escapes.

When war am over he won't free me, says I'm valuable to him in his trade. He say, "Nigger, you's supposed to be free but I'll pay you a dollar a week and if you runs off I'll kill you." So he makes me do like before the War, but gives me about a dollar a month, 'stead week. He says I cost more'n I'm worth, but he won't let me go. Times I don't know why I didn't die before I'm growed, sleepin' on the ground, winter and summer, rain and snow. But not much snow there.

Master helt me long years after the War. If anybody get after him, he told them I stay 'cause I wants to stay, but told me if I left he'd kill him another nigger. I stayed till he gits in a drunk brawl one night with men and women and they gits to shootin' and some kilt. Master got kilt.

Then I'm left to live or die, so I wanders from place to place. I nearly starved to death before I'd leave New Orleans, 'cause I couldn't think Master am dead and I afraid. Finally I gets up nerve to leave town and stays the first night in white man's barn. I never slept. Every time I hears something I jumps up and Master be standin' there, lookin' at me, but soon's I get up he'd leave.

Next night I slept out in a hay field, and Master he get right top of a tree and start hollerin' at me. I never stays in that place. I gets gone from that place. I gets back to town fast as my legs carry me.

Then I gets locked up in jail. I didn't know what for, never did know. One the men says to me to come with him and takes me to the woods and gives me an ax. I cuts rails till I nearly falls, all with chain locked round feet, so I couldn't run off. He turns me loose and I wanders again. Never had a home. Works for men long 'nough to get fifty, sixty cents, then starts roamin' again, like a stray dog.

After long time I marries Feline Graham. Then I has a home and we has a white preacher marry us. We has one boy and he farms and I lives with him. I worked at sawmill and farms all my life, but never could make much money.

You know, the nigger was wild till the white man made what he has out of the nigger. He done educate them real smart.

BOSTON BLACKWELL

Interviewed at North Little Rock, Arkansas
Interviewed by Beulah Sherwood Hagg
Age when interviewed: 98

I KNOWS my age, good. Old Miss, she told me when I got sold—"Boss, you is thirteen—borned Christmas. Be sure to tell your new mistress and she put you down in her book." My borned name was Pruitt 'cause I got borned on Robert Pruitt's plantation in Georgia—Franklin County, Georgia. But Blackwell is my freed name. You see, after my mammy got sold down to Augusta—I wished I could tell you the man what brought her; I ain't never seed him since—I was sold to go to Arkansas, Jefferson County, Arkansas. Then was when Old Miss telled me I am thirteen. It was before the Civil War I come here. The onliest auction of slaves I ever seed was in Memphis, coming on to Arkansas. I heered a girl bid off for eight hundred dollars. She was about fifteen, I reckon. I heered a woman—a breeding woman—bid off for fifteen hundred dollars. They always brought good money. I'm telling you, it was when we was coming from Atlanta.

I'll tell you how I runned away and joined the Yankees. You know Abraham Lincoln declared freedom in '63, first day of January. In October '63, I runned away and went to Pine Bluff to get to the Yankees. I was on the Blackwell plantation south of Pine Bluff in '68. They was building a new house; I wanted to feel some putty in my hand. One early morning I climb a ladder to get a little chunk and the overseer man, he seed me. Here he come, yelling me to get down; he gwine whip me 'cause I'se a thief, he say. He call a slave boy and tell him cut ten willer whips; he gwine wear every one out on me. When he's gone to eat breakfast, I runs to my cabin and tells my sister, "I'se leaving this here place for good." She cry and say, "Overseer man, he kill you." I says, "He kill me anyhow." The young boy what cut the whips—he named Jerry—he come along with me, and we wade the stream for long piece. Heered the hounds a-howling, getting ready for to chase us. Then we hide in dark woods. It was cold, frosty weather.

11

Two days and two nights we traveled. That boy, he so cold and hungry, he want to fall out by the way, but I drug him on. When we gets to the Yankee camp all our troubles was over. We gets all the contraband we could eat. They was hundreds of runaways there. The Yankees feeds all them refugees on contraband. They made me a driver of a team in the quartermaster's department. I was always careful to do everything they told me. They told me I was free when I gets to the Yankee camp, but I couldn't go outside much. Iffen you could get to the Yankee's camp you was free right now.

That old story about forty acres and a mule, it make me laugh. They sure did tell us that, but I never knowed any person which got it. The officers told us we would all get slave pension. That just exactly what they tell. They sure did tell me I would get a parcel of ground to farm. Nothing ever hatched out of that, neither.

When I got to Pine Bluff I stayed contraband. When the battle come, Captain Manly carried me down to the battleground and I stay there till fighting was over. I was a soldier that day. I didn't shoot no gun nor cannon. I carried water from the river for to put out the fire in the cotton bales what made the breastworks. Every time the 'Federates shoot, the cotton, it come on fire. So after the battle, they transfer me back to quartermaster driver. Captain Dodridge was his name. I served in Little Rock under Captain Haskell. I was swored in for during the War. It was on the corner of Main and Markham Street in Little Rock I was swored in. Year of '64. I was 5 feet, 8 inches high. Living in the army was purty good. Iffen you obeyed them Yankee officers they treated you purty good, but iffen you didn't they sure went rough on you.

After the soldiers all go away, the first thing, I work on the railroad. They was just beginning to come here. I digged pits out, going along front of where the tracks was to go. I get one dollar a day. I felt like the richest man in the world! I boarded with a white family. Always I was a-watching for my slave pension to begin coming. Before I left the army my captain, he told me to file. My file number, it is 1,115,857. After I keeped them papers for so many years, white and black folks both told me it ain't never coming—my slave pension—and I reckon the children tored up the papers. That number for me is filed in Washington.

After the railroad I went steamboating. First one was a little one; they call her *Fort Smith* 'cause she go from Little Rock to Fort Smith. It was funny, too, her captain was name Smith. Captain Eugene Smith was his name. He was good, but the mate was sure rough. They's plenty to do on a riverboat. Never is no time for rest. Load, unload, scrub. Just you do whatever you is told to do and do it right now, and you'll keep outen trouble, on a steamboat, or a railroad, or in the army, or wherever you is. That's what I knows.

I reckon they was right smart old masters what didn't want to let they slaves go after freedom. They hated to turn them loose. Just let them work on. Heap of them didn't know freedom come. I used to hear tell how the government had to send soldiers away down in the far back country to make them turn the slaves loose. I can't tell you how them free niggers was living; I was too busy looking out for myself. Heaps of them went to farming. They was sharecroppers.

Them Ku Kluxers was terrible—what they done to people. Oh, God, they was bad. They come sneaking up and runned you outen your house and take everything you had. They was rough on the women and children. People all wanted to stay close by where soldiers was. I sure knowed they was my friend.

After peace, I got with my sister. She's the onliest of all my people I ever seed again. She telled me she was scared all that day I runned away. She couldn't work, she shake so bad. She heered overseer man getting ready to chase me and Jerry. He saddle his horse, take his gun and pistol, both. He gwine kill me on sight, but Jerry, he say he bring him back, dead or alive, tied to his horse's tail. But he didn't get us, ha, ha, ha. Yankees got us.

Now you wants to know about this voting business. I voted for General Grant. Army men come around and registered you before voting time. It wasn't no trouble to vote them days; white and black all voted together. All you had to do was tell who you was vote for and they give you a colored ticket. All the men up had different colored tickets. Iffen you're voting for Grant, you get his color. It was easy. They was colored men in office, plenty. Colored legislators, and colored circuit clerks, and colored county clerks. They sure was some big officers colored in them times. They was all my friends. This here used to be a good county, but I tell you it sure is tough now. I think it's wrong—exactly wrong that we can't vote now. The Jim Crow law, it put us out. The Constitution of the United States, it give us the right to vote. It made us citizens, it did.

You just keeps on asking about me, lady. I ain't never been asked about myself in my *whole* life! Now you wants to know after railroading and steamboating what. They was still work the Yankee army wanted done. The War had been gone for long time. All over every place was bodies buried. They was bringing them to Little Rock to put in government graveyard. They sent me all over the state to help bring them here. Major Forsythe was my quartermaster then.

After that was done, they put me to work at St. John's hospital. The work I done there liked to ruin me for life. I cleaned out the water closets. After a while I took down sick from the work—the scent, you know—but I keep on till I get so far gone I can't stay on my feets no more. A misery got me in the chest; right here, and it been with me all through life; it with me now.

I filed for a pension on this ailment. I never did get it. The government never took care of me like it did some soldiers. They said I was not an enlisted man, that I was a employed man, so I couldn't get no pension. I give my whole life to the government for many years. White and black both always telling me I should have a pension. I stood on the battlefield just like other soldiers. Iffen I could of had some help when I been sick, I might not be so no account now.

W. L. BOST

Interviewed at Asheville, North Carolina
Interviewed by Marjorie Jones
Age when interviewed: 88

MY MASSA'S name was Jonas Bost. He had a hotel in Newton, North Carolina. My mother and grandmother both belonged to the Bost family. My ole massa had two large plantations, one about three miles from Newton and another four miles away. It took a lot of niggers to keep work a-goin' on them both. The womenfolks had to work in the hotel and in the Big House in town. Ole Missus she was a good woman. She never allowed the massa to buy or sell any slaves. There never was an overseer on the whole plantation. The oldest colored man always looked after the niggers. We niggers lived better than the niggers on the other plantations.

I remember when I was a little boy, about ten years, the speculators come through Newton with droves of slaves. They always stay at our place. The poor critters nearly froze to death. They always come 'long on the last of December so that the niggers would be ready for sale on the first day of January. Many the time I see four or five of them chained together. They never had enough clothes on to keep a cat warm. The women never wore anything but a thin dress and a petticoat and one underwear. I've seen the ice balls hangin' on to the bottom of their dresses as they ran along, just like sheep in a pasture before they are sheared. They never wore any shoes. Just run along on the ground, all spewed up with ice. The speculators always rode on horses and drove the poor niggers. When they get cold, they make 'em run till they are warm again.

The speculators stayed in the hotel and put the niggers in the quarters just like droves of hogs. All through the night I could hear them mournin' and prayin'. I didn't know the Lord would let people live who were so cruel. The gates were always locked and they was a guard on the outside to shoot anyone who tried to run away. Them slaves look just like droves of turkey runnin' along in front of them horses.

15

I remember when they put 'em on the block to sell 'em. The ones 'tween eighteen and thirty always bring the most money. The auctioneer he stand off at a distance and cry 'em off as they stand on the block. I can hear his voice as long as I live.

If the one they going to sell was a young Negro man this is what he says: "Now gentlemen and fellow citizens here is a big black buck Negro. He's stout as a mule. Good for any kind o' work and he never gives any trouble. How much am I offered for him?" And then the sale would commence and the nigger would be sold to the highest bidder.

If they put up a young nigger woman, the auctioneer cry out: "Here's a young nigger wench, how much am I offered for her?" The poor thing stand on the block a shiverin' and a shakin' nearly froze to death. The poor mothers beg the speculators to sell 'em with their husbands, but the speculator only take what he want. So maybe the poor thing never see her husband again.

Ole Massa always see that we get plenty to eat. O' course it was no fancy rations. Just corn bread, milk, fat meat, and 'lasses, but the Lord knows that was lots more than other poor niggers got. Some of them had such bad masters.

Us poor niggers never allowed to learn anything. All the readin' they ever hear was when they was carried through the big Bible. The massa say that keep the slaves in they places. They was one nigger boy in Newton who was terrible smart. He learn to read and write. He take other colored children out in the fields and teach 'em about the Bible, but they forget it before the next Sunday.

Then the patterrollers they keep close watch on the poor niggers so they have no chance to do anything or go anywhere. They just like policemen, only worser, 'cause they never let the niggers go anywhere without a pass from his master. If you wasn't in your proper place when the patterrollers come they lash you till you was black and blue. The women got fifteen lashes and the men thirty. That is for just bein' out without a pass. If the nigger done anything worse he was taken to the jail and put in the whippin' post. They was two holes cut for the arms stretch up in the air and a block to put your feet in, then they whip you with cowhide whip. And the clothes sure never get any of them licks.

I remember how they kill one nigger whippin' him with the bullwhip. Many the poor nigger nearly killed with the bullwhip. But this one die. He was a stubborn Negro and didn't do as much work as his massa thought he ought to. He been lashed lot before. So they take him to the whippin' post, and then they strip his clothes off and then the man stand off and cut him with the whip. His back was cut all to pieces. The cuts about half inch apart. Then after they whip him they tie him down and put salt on him. Then after he lie in the sun awhile they whip him agin. But when they finish with he, he was dead.

Plenty of the colored woman have children by the white men. She know better than to not do what he say. Didn't have much of that until the men from South Carolina come up here and settle and bring slaves. Then they take them very same children what have they own blood and make slaves out of them. If the missus find out she raise revolution. But she hardly find out. The white men not going to tell and the nigger women were always afraid to. So they just go on hopin' that things won't be that way always.

I remember how the driver, he was the man who did most of the whippin', used to whip some of the niggers. He would tie their hands together and then put their hands down over their knees, then take a stick and stick it 'tween they hands and knees. Then he take hold of them and beat 'em first on one side, then on the other.

Us niggers never have chance to go to Sunday school and church. The white folks feared for niggers to get any religion and education, but I reckon somethin' inside just told us about God and that there was a better place hereafter. We would sneak off and have prayer meetin'. Sometimes the patterrollers catch us and beat us good but that didn't keep us from tryin'. I remember one old song we used to sing when we meet down in the woods back of the barn. My mother she sing and pray to the Lord to deliver us out o' slavery. She always say she thankful she was never sold from her children, and that our massa not so mean as some of the others. But the old song it went something like this:

Oh, Mother let's go down, let's go down, let's go down, let's go down.
Oh, Mother let's go down, down in the valley to pray.
As I went down in the valley to pray,
Studyin' about that good ole way,
Who shall wear that starry crown?
Good Lord, show me the way.

Then the other part was just like that except it said "Father" instead of "Mother," and then "Sister" and then "Brother." Then they sing sometime:

We camp awhile in the wilderness, in the wilderness, in the wilderness.
We camp awhile in the wilderness, where the Lord makes me happy,
And then I'm a-goin' home.

I don't remember much about the War. There was no fightin' done in Newton. Just a skirmish or two. Most of the people get everything just ready to run when the Yankee soldiers come through the town. This was toward the last of the War. 'Course the niggers knew what all the fightin' was about, but they didn't dare say anything. The man who owned the slaves was too mad as it was, and if the niggers said anything they get shot right then and there. The soldiers tell us after the War that we get food, clothes, and wages from our massas else we leave. But they was very few that ever got anything. Our ole massa say he not gwine pay us anything. 'Course his money was no good, but he wouldn't pay us if it had been.

Then the Ku Klux Klan came along. They were terrible dangerous. They wear long gowns, touch the ground. They ride horses through the town at night and if they find a Negro that tries to get nervy or have a little bit for himself, they lash him nearly to death and gag him and leave him to do the best he can. Sometime they put sticks in the top of the tall thing they wear and then put an extra head up there with scary eyes and great big mouth. Then they stick it clear up in the air to scare the poor Negroes to death.

They had another thing they call the "Donkey Devil" that was just as bad. They take the skin of a donkey and get inside of it and run after the poor Negroes. Them was bad times, them was bad times. I know folks think the books tell the truth but they sure don't. Us poor niggers had to take it all.

Then after the War was over we was afraid to move. Just like tarpins or turtles after 'mancipation. Just stick our heads out to see how the land lay. My mammy stay with Marse Jonah for about a year after freedom, then Ole Solomon Hall made her an offer. Ole man Hall was a good man if there ever was one. He freed all of his slaves about two years before 'mancipation and gave each of them so much money when he died; that is, he put that in his will. But when he die his sons and daughters never give anything to the poor Negroes.

My mother went to live with on the place belongin' to the nephew of Solomon Hall. All of her six children went with her. Mother she cook for the white folks and the children make crop. When the first year was up us children got the first money we had in our lives. My mother certainly was happy.

We live on this place for over four years. When I was about twenty year old I married a girl from West Virginia, but she didn't live but just about a year. I stayed down there for a year or so and then I met Mamie. We came here and both of us went to work. We work at the same place.

We bought this little piece of ground about forty-two years ago. We gave one hundred twenty-five dollars for it. We had to buy the lumber to build the house a little at a time but finally we got the house done. It's been a good home for us and the children.

We have two daughters and one adopted son. Both of the girls are good cooks. One of them lives in New Jersey and cooks in a big hotel. She and her husband come to see us about once a year. But the adopted boy, he was part white. We took him when he was small and did the best we could by him. He never did like to associate with colored people. I remember one time when he was a small child I took him to town and the conductor made me put him in the front of the streetcar 'cause he thought I was just caring for him and that he was a white boy. Well, we sent him to school until he finished. Then he joined the navy. I ain't seen him in several years. The last letter I got from him he say he ain't spoke to a colored girl since he has been there. This made me mad so I took his insurance policy and cashed it. I didn't want nothin' to do with him, if he deny his own color.

JULIA BROWN

Interviewed at Atlanta, Georgia
Interviewed by Geneva Tonsill
Age when interviewed: 85

I WAS born four miles from Commerce, Georgia, and was thirteen year old at surrender. I belonged to the Nash family—three old maid sisters. My mama belonged to the Nashes and my papa belonged to General Burns; he was a officer in the War. There was six of us chillens, Lucy, Melvina, Johnnie, Callie, Joe, and me. We didn't stay together long, as we was give out to different people. The Nashes didn't believe in selling slaves and we was known as their niggers. They sold one once 'cause the other slaves said they would kill him 'cause he had a baby by his own daughter. So to keep him from bein' kilt, they sold him.

My mama died the year of surrender. I didn't fare well after her death. I had such a hard time. I was give to the Mitchell family and they done every cruel thing they could to me. I slept on the floor nine years, winter and summer, sick or well. I never wore anything but a cotton dress, a shimmy, and drawers. That woman didn't care what happened to the niggers. Sometime she would take us to church. We'd walk to the church house. I never went nowhere else. That woman took delight in callin' slaves. She'd lash us with a cowhide whip. I had to shift for myself.

They didn't mind the slaves matin', but they wanted their niggers to marry only amongst them on their place. They didn't allow 'em to mate with other slaves from other places. When the women had babies they was treated kind and they let 'em stay in. We called it "lay-in," just about like they do now. We didn't go to no hospitals as they do now. We just had our babies and a granny to catch 'em. We didn't have all the pain-easin' medicines then. The granny would put a rusty piece of tin or a ax under the mattress and this would ease the pain. The granny put a ax under my mattress once. This was to cut off the after-pains and it sure did, too. We'd set up the fifth day and after the "layin-in" time was up we was allowed to walk outdoors and they told us to walk around the house just once and come in the house. This was to keep us from takin' a 'lapse.

20

We wasn't allowed to go around and have pleasure as the folks does today. We had to have passes to go wherever we wanted. When we'd get out there was a bunch of white men called the "patty rollers." They'd come in and see if all us had passes, and if they found any who didn't have a pass, he was whipped, give fifty or more lashes—and they'd count them lashes. If they said a hundred, you got a hundred. They was somethin' like the Klu Klux. We was 'fraid to tell our masters about the patty rollers because we was scared they'd whip us again, for we was told not to tell. They'd sing a little ditty; it went somethin' like this:

> Run, nigger, run. De patty rollers'll get you.
> Run, nigger, run. You'd better get away.

We was 'fraid to go any place.

Slaves was treated in most cases like cattle. A man went about the country buyin' up slaves like buyin' up cattle and the like, and he was called a "speculator." Then he'd sell 'em to the highest bidder. Oh! it was pitiful to see chillen taken from their mothers' breasts, mothers sold, husbands sold from wives. One woman he was to buy had a baby, and of course the baby come before he bought her and he wouldn't buy the baby, said he hadn't bargained to buy the baby, too, and he just wouldn't.

My uncle was married, but he was owned by one master and his wife was owned by another. He was allowed to visit his wife on Wednesday and Saturday, that's the onliest time he could get off. He went on Wednesday and when he went back on Saturday his wife had been bought by the speculator and he never did know where she was.

I worked hard always. You can't imagine what a hard time I had. I split rails like a man. I used a huge glut and a iron wedge drove into the wood with a maul, and this would split the wood. I help spin the cotton into thread for our clothes. The thread was made into big broaches—four broaches made four cuts, or one hank. After the thread was made we used a loom to weave the cloth. We had no sewin' machine—had to sew by hand. My mistress had a big silver bird and she would always catch the cloth in the bird's bill and this would hold it for her to sew.

I didn't get to handle money when I was young. I worked from sunup to sundown. We never had overseers like some of the slaves. We was give so much work to do in a day and if the white folks went off on a vacation they would give us so much work to do while they was gone and we better have all of that done, too, when they'd come home.

They made me hoe when I was a child and I'd keep right up with the others, 'cause they'd tell me that if I got behind a runaway nigger would get me and split open my head and get the milk outen it. Of course, I didn't know then that weren't true. I believed everything they told me and that made me work the harder.

Some of the white folks was very kind to their slaves. Some did not believe in slavery and some freed them before the War and even give 'em land and homes. Some would give the niggers meal, lard, and like that.

There was a white man, Mister Jim, that was very mean to the slaves. He'd go round and beat 'em. He'd even go to the little homes, tear down the chimneys, and do all sorts of cruel things. The chimneys was made of mud and straw and sticks; they was powerful strong, too. Mister Jim was just a mean man, and when he died we all said God got tired of Mister Jim being so mean and kilt him.

When they laid him out on the coolin' board, everybody was settin' round, moanin' over his death, and all of a sudden Mister Jim rolled offen the coolin' board. Such a-runnin' and gettin' outen that room you never saw! We said Mister Jim was tryin' to run the niggers and we was 'fraid to go about at night. I believe it then. Now that they's embalmin' I know that must have been gas and he was purgin', for they didn't know nothin' about embalmin' then. They didn't keep dead folks outen the ground long in them days.

Doctors wasn't so plentiful then. They'd go round in buggies and on hosses. Them that rode on a hoss had saddle pockets just filled with little bottles and lots of them. He'd try one medicine and if it didn't do no good he'd try another until it did do good. And when the doctor went to see a sick person he'd stay right there until he was better. He didn't just come in and write a prescription for somebody to take to a drugstore.

We used herbs a lot in them days. When a body had dropsy we'd set him in a tepid bath made of mullein leaves. There was a jimsonweed we'd use for rheumatism, and for asthma we'd use tea made of chestnut leaves. We'd get the chestnut leaves, dry them in the sun just like tea leaves, and we wouldn't let them leaves get wet for nothin' in the world while they was dryin'. We'd take poke collard roots, boil them, and then take sugar and make a syrup. This was the best thing for asthma. It was known to cure it, too. For colds and such we used horehound; made candy outen it with brown sugar. We used a lots of rock candy and whiskey for colds, too. They had a remedy that they used for consumption—take dry cow manure, make a tea of this, and flavor it with mint and give it to the sick person. We didn't need many doctors then for we didn't have so much sickness in them days, and naturally they didn't die so fast. Folks lived a long time then. They used a lot of peach tree leaves, too, for fever, and when the stomach got upset we'd crush the leaves, pour water over them, and wouldn't let them drink any other kind of water till they was better. I still believes in them old home-made medicines, too, and I don't believe in so many doctors.

We didn't have stoves plentiful then; just ovens we set in the fire-place. I'se toted a many a armful of bark—good old hickory bark to cook with. We'd cook light bread—both flour and corn. The yeast for this bread was made from hops. Coals of fire was put on top of the oven and under the bottom, too. Everything was cooked on coals from a wood fire—coffee and all. The victuals was good in them days. We got our vegetables outen the garden in season and didn't have all the hot-house vegetables. There was racks fitted in the fireplace to put pots on. Once there was a big pot settin' on the fire, just boilin' away with a big roast in it. As the water boiled, the meat turned over and over, comin' up to the top and goin' down again. Old Sandy, the dog, come into the kitchen. He set there awhile and watched that meat roll over and over in the pot, and all of a sudden-like he grabbed at that meat and pulls it outen the pot. Course he couldn't eat it 'cause it was hot and they got the meat before he et it.

The kitchen was away from the Big House, so the victuals was cooked and carried up to the house. I'd carry it up myself. We couldn't eat all the different kinds of victuals the white folks et and one mornin' when I was carryin' the breakfast to the Big House we had waffles that was a pretty golden brown and pipin' hot. They was a picture to look at and I just couldn't keep from takin' one, and that was the hardest waf-fle for me to eat before I got to the Big House I ever saw. I just couldn't get rid of that waffle 'cause my conscience whipped me so.

They taught me to do everything. I'd use battlin' blocks and battlin' sticks to wash the clothes. We all did. The clothes was taken out of the water and put on the block and beat with a battlin' stick, which was made like a paddle. On wash days you could hear them battlin' sticks poundin' every which way. We made our own soap, used old meat and grease, and poured water over wood ashes which was kept in a rack-like thing, and the water would drip through the ashes. This made strong lye. We used a lot of such lye, too, to boil with.

Sometimes the slaves would run away. Their masters was mean to them that caused them to run away. Sometimes they would live in caves. They got along all right—what with other people slippin' things into 'em. And, too, they'd steal hogs, chickens, and anything else they could get their hands on. Some white people would help, too, for there was some white people who didn't believe in slavery.

They would always try to find them slaves that run away, and if they was found they'd be beat or sold to somebody else. My grandmother run away from her master. She stayed in the woods and she washed her clothes in the branches. She used sand for soap.

I stayed with the Mitchells till Miss Hannah died. I even helped to lay her out. I didn't go to the graveyard, though. I didn't have a home after she died and I wandered from place to place, stayin' with a white family this time and then a nigger family the next time. I moved to Jackson County and stayed with a Mister Frank Dowdy. I didn't stay there long, though. Then I moved to Winder, Georgia. They called it "Jug Tavern" in them days, 'cause jugs was made there.

I married Green Hinton in Winder. Got along well after marryin' him. He farmed for a livin' and made a good livin' for me and the eight chillens, all born in Winder. The chillens was grown nearly when he died and was able to help me with the smallest ones. I got along all right after his death and didn't have such a hard time raisin' the chillens. Then I married Jim Brown and moved to Atlanta. Jim farmed at first for a livin' and then he worked on the railroad—the seaboard. He helped to grade the first railroad track for that line. He was a sand-dryer.

After he moved here he bought this home. I'se lived here twenty years. Jim was killed on the railroad. He was comin' in the railroad yard one day and stepped off the little engine they used for the workers right in the path of the L & N train. He was cut up and crushed to pieces. He didn't have a sign of a head. They used a rake to get up the pieces they did get. A man brought a few pieces out here in a bundle and I wouldn't even look at them.

I got a little money from the railroad, but the lawyer got most of it. He brought me a few dollars out and told me not to discuss it with anyone nor tell how much I got. I tried to get some of the men that worked with him to tell me just how it all happened, but they wouldn't talk, and it was scandalous how them niggers held their peace and wouldn't tell me anything. The boss man came out later but he didn't seem interested in it at all, so I got little or nothing for his death. The lawyer got it for hisself.

ANTHONY DAWSON

Interviewed at Tulsa, Oklahoma
Interviewer not identified
Age when interviewed: 105

> Run nigger, run,
> De Patteroll get you!
> Run nigger, run,
> De Patteroll come!
> Watch nigger, watch,
> De Patteroll trick you!
> Watch nigger, watch,
> He got a big gun!

DAT ONE of the songs de slaves all knowed, and de children down on de "twenty acres" used to sing it when dey playing in de moonlight round de cabins in de quarters. Sometime I wonder iffen de white folks didn't make dat song up so us niggers would keep in line.

None of my old master's boys tried to get away 'cepting two, and dey met up with evil, both of 'em. One of dem niggers was fetching a bull-tongue from a piece of new ground way at de back of de plantation and bringing it to my pappy to get it sharped. My pappy was de blacksmith. Dis boy got out in de big road to walk in de soft sand, and 'long come a wagon with a white overseer and five, six niggers going somewhere. Dey stopped and told dat boy to get in and ride. Dat was de last anybody seen him.

Dat overseer and another one was cotched after awhile and showed up to be underground railroaders. Dey would take a bunch of niggers into town for some excuse and on de way just pick up a extra nigger and show him where to go to get on de "railroad system." When de runaway niggers got to de North dey had to go in de army, and dat boy from our place got killed. He was a good boy, but dey just talked him into it. Dem railroaders was honest, and dey didn't take no presents, but de patrollers was low white trash! We all knowed dat if a patroller just rode right by and didn't say nothing dat he was doing his honest job, but

25

iffen he stopped his hoss and talked to a nigger he was after some kind of trade.

Dat other black boy was hoeing cotton way in de back of de field and de patroller rid up and down de big road, saying nothing to nobody. De next day another white man was on de job, and 'long in de evening a man come by and axed de niggers about de fishing and hunting! Dat black boy seen he was de same man what was riding de day before and he knowed it was a underground trick. But he didn't see all de trick, bless God!

We found out afterwards dat he told his mammy about it. She worked at de Big House and she stole something for him to give dat low white trash I reckon, 'cause de next day he played sick along in de evening and de black overlooker—he was my uncle—sent him back to de quarters. He never did get there, but when dey started de hunt dey found him about a mile away in de woods with his head shot off, and Old Master sold his mammy to a trader right away. He never whipped his grown niggers.

Dat was de way it worked. Dey was all kinds of white folks just like dey is now. One man in Sesesh clothes would shoot you if you tried to run away. Maybe another Sesesh would help slip you out to the underground and say "God bless you, poor black devil," and some of dem dat was poor would help you if you could bring 'em somethin' you stole, like a silver dish or spoons or a couple big hams. I couldn't blame them poor white folks, with the men in the War and the women and children hungry. The niggers didn't belong to them nohow, and they had to live somehow. But now and then they was a devil on earth, walking in the sight of God and spreading iniquity before him. He was de low-down Sesesh dat would take what a poor runaway nigger had to give for his chance to get away, and den give him 'structions dat would lead him right into de hands of de patrollers and get him caught or shot. Yes, dat's de way it was. Devils and good people walking in de road at de same time, and nobody could tell one from t'other.

I remember about de trickery so good 'cause I was "grown and out" at that time. When I was a little boy I was a house boy, 'cause my mammy was the house woman, but when the War broke I already been sent to the fields and Mammy was still at de house. I was born on July 25, 1832. I know, 'cause Old Master keep de book on his slaves just like on his own family. I was born on the plantation, soon after my pappy and mammy was brought to it. I don't remember whether they was bought or come from my mistress' father. He was mighty rich and had several hundred niggers. When she was married he give her forty niggers. One of them was my pappy's brother. His name was John, and he was my master's overlooker. We called a white man boss the "overseer," but a nigger was a overlooker. John could read and write and figger, and Old Master didn't have no white overseer.

Master was a good man, and Old Mistress was de best woman in de world! Master's name was Levi Dawson, and his plantation was eighteen miles east of Greenville, North Carolina. De plantation had more than five hundred acres and most was in cotton and tobacco. But we raised corn and oats, and lots of cattle and horses, and plenty of sheep for wool. It was a beautiful place, with all the fences around the Big House and along the front made out of barked poles, rider style, and all whitewashed. The Big House set back from the big road about a quarter of a mile. It was only one story, but it had lots of rooms. There was four rooms in a bunch on one side and four in a bunch on the other, with a wide hall in between. They was made of square adzed logs all weatherboarded on the outside and planked up and plastered on the inside. Then they was a long gallery clean across the front with big pillars made out of bricks and plastered over. They called it the passage 'cause it didn't have no floor excepting bricks, and a buggy could drive right under it. Mostly it was used to set under talk and play cards and drink the best whiskey Old Master could buy. Back in behind the Big House was the kitchen, and the smokehouse in another place made of plank, and all was whitewashed and painted white all the time.

Old Mistress was named Miss Susie and she was born an Isley. She brought forty niggers from her pappy as a present, and Master Levi just had four or five, but he had got all his land from his pappy. She had the niggers and he had the land. That's the way it was, and that's the way it stayed! She never let him punish one of her niggers and he never asked her about buying or selling land. Her pappy was richer than his pappy, and she was sure quality!

My pappy's name was Anthony, and Mammy's name was Chanie. He was the blacksmith and fixed the wagons, but he couldn't read and figger like Uncle John. Mammy was the head house woman but didn't know any letters either. They was both black like me. Old man Isley, where they come from, had lots of niggers, but I don't think they was off the boat.

Master Levi had three sons and no daughters. The oldest son was Simeon. He was in the Sesesh army. The other two boys was too young. I can't remember their names. They was a lot younger and I was grown and out before they got big.

Old Master was a fine Christian but he like his juleps anyways. He let us niggers have preachings and prayers and would give us a parole to go ten or fifteen miles to a camp meeting and stay two or three days with nobody but Uncle John to stand for us. Mostly we had white preachers, but when we had a black preacher that was heaven. We didn't have no voodoo women nor conjure folks at our "twenty acres." We all knowed about the Word and the unseen Son of God and we didn't put no stock in conjure. 'Course we had luck charms and good and bad signs, but everybody got dem things, even nowadays. My boy had a white officer in the Big War and he tells me that man had a li'l old doll tied around his wrist on a gold chain.

We used herbs and roots for common ailments, like sassafrass and boneset and peach tree poultices and coon rot tea, but when a nigger got bad sick Old Master sent for a white doctor. I remember that old doctor. He lived in Greenville and he had to come eighteen miles in a buggy. When he give some nigger medicine he would be afraid the nigger was like lots of them that believed in conjure, and he would say, "If you don't take that medicine like I tell you and I have to come back here to see you I going to break your damn neck next time I come out here!" When it was bad weather sometime the black boy sent after him had to carry a lantern to show him the way back. If that nigger on his mule got too far ahead so old doctor couldn't see de light he sure catch de devil from that old doctor and from Old Master, too, lessen he was one of Old Missy's house niggers, and then Old Master just grumble to satisfy the doctor.

Down in the quarters we had the spinning house, where the old woman card the wool and run the loom. They made double weave for the winter time, and all the white folks and slaves had good clothes and good food.

Master made us all eat all we could hold. He would come to the smokehouse and look in and say, "You niggers ain't cutting down that smoke side and that souse like you ought to! You made dat meat and you got to help eat it up!"

Never no work on Sunday 'cepting the regular chores. The overlooker made everybody clean up and wash de children up, and after the praying we had games—antny over and marbles and "I Spy" and de likes of that. Sometimes de boys would go down in de woods and get a possum. I love possum and sweet 'taters, but de coon meat more delicate and de hair don't stink up de meat.

I wasn't at the quarters much as a boy. I was at the Big House with my mammy, and I had to swing the fly brush over my old mistress when she was sewing or eating or taking her nap. Sometime I would keep the flies offen Old Master, and when I would get tired and let the brush slap his neck he would kick at me and cuss me, but he never did reach me. He had a way of keeping us little niggers scared to death and never hurting nobody.

I was down in the field burning brush when I first heard the guns in the War. De fighting was de battle at Kingston, North Carolina, and it lasted four days and nights. After while bunches of Sesesh come riding by hauling wounded people in wagons, and then pretty soon big bunches of Yankees come by, but dey didn't act like dey was trying very hard to catch up.

Dey had de country in charge quite some time, and they had forages coming round all the time. By dat time Old Master done buried his money and all de silver and de big clock, but the Yankees didn't appear to search out dat kind of stuff. All dey ask about was did anybody find a bottle of brandy!

When de War ended up most all de niggers stay with Old Master and work on de shares, until de land get divided up and sold off and the young niggers get scattered to town.

I never did have no truck with de Ku Kluckers, but I had to step mighty high to keep outen it! De sure 'nough Kluxes never did bother around us 'cause we minded our own business and never give no trouble. We wouldn't let no niggers come round our place talking about delegates and voting, and we just all stayed on the place. But dey was some low white trash and some devilish niggers made out like dey was Ku Klux ranging round de country stealing hosses and taking things. Old Master said dey wasn't sure 'nough, so I reckon he knowed who the regular ones was.

These bunches that come around robbing got into our neighborhood and Old Master told me I better not have my old horse at the house, 'cause if I had him they would know nobody had been there stealing and it wouldn't do no good to hide anything 'cause they would tear up the place hunting what I had and maybe whip or kill me. "Your old hoss ain't no good, Tony, and you better kill him to make them think you already been raided on," Old Master told me, so I led him out and knocked him in the head with an ax, and then we hid all our grub and waited for Kluckers to come most any night, but they never did come. I borried a hoss to use in the day and took him back home every night for about a year.

The niggers kept talking about being free, but they wasn't free then and they ain't now. Putting them free just like putting goat hair on a sheep. When it rain de goat come a-running and get in de shelter, 'cause his hair won't shed the rain and he get cold, but de sheep ain't got sense enough to get in the shelter but just stand out and let it rain on him all day. But the good Lord fix the sheep up with a woolly jacket that turn the water off, and he don't get cold, so he don't have to have no brains. De nigger during slavery was like de sheep. He couldn't take care of hisself but his master looked out for him, and he didn't have to use his brains. De master's protection was like de woolly coat. But de 'mancipation come and take off de woolly coat and leave de nigger with no protection and he cain't take care of hisself either.

When de niggers was set free lots of them got mighty uppity, and everybody wanted to be a delegate to something or other. The Yankees told us we could go down and vote in the 'lections and our color was good enough to run for anything. Heaps of niggers believed them. You cain't fault them for that, 'cause they didn't have no better sense, but I knowed the black folks didn't have no business mixing in until they knowed more. It was a long time after the War before I went down to vote and everything quiet by that time, but I heard people talk about the fights at the schoolhouse when they had the first election.

I just stayed on around the old place a long time, and then I got on another piece of ground and farmed, not far from Greenville, until 1900. Then I moved to Hearn, Texas, and stayed with my son Ed until 1903 when we moved to Sapulpa in the Creek Nation. We come to Tulsa several years ago, and I been living with him ever since.

MILLIE EVANS

Interviewed at El Dorado, Arkansas
Interviewed by Mrs. Carol Graham
Age when interviewed: 88

I WAS born in 1849, but I don't know just when. My birthday comes in fodder pullin' time cause my ma said she was pullin' up till 'bout a hour 'fore I was born. Was born in North Carolina and was a young lady at de time of surrender.

I don't remember Old Master's name; all I remember is dat we call dem Old Master and Old Mistress. Dey had 'bout a hundred niggers, and dey was rich. Master always tended de men and Mistress tended to us.

Every mornin' 'bout four o'clock Old Master would ring de bell for us to get up by, and you could hear dat bell ringin' all over de plantation. I can hear it now. It would go ting-a-ling, ting-a-ling, and I can see dem now stirrin' in Carolina. I get so lonesome when I thinks 'bout times we used to have. 'Twas better livin' back yonder dan now.

I stayed with my ma every night, but my mistress raised me. My ma had to work hard, so every time Old Mistress thought we little black chilluns was hungry between meals she would call us up to de house to eat. Sometimes she would give us johnnycake and plenty of buttermilk to drink with it. Dey had a long trough for us dat dey would keep so clean. Dey would fill this trough with buttermilk, and all us children would get around de trough and drink with our mouths and hold our johnnycake with our hands. I can just see myself drinkin' now. It was so good. Dere was so many black folks to cook for dat de cookin' was done outdoors. Greens was cooked in a big black wash pot just like you boils clothes in now. And sometime dey would crumble bread in de pot likker and give us spoons, and we would stand around de pot and eat. When we ate our regular meals de table was set under a chinaberry tree with a oilcloth tablecloth, and when dey called us to de table dey would rin' de bell. But we didn't eat out of plates. We ate out of gourds and had homemade wood spoons. And we had plenty to eat. Whoooeee! Just plenty to eat. Old Master's folks raised plenty of meat,

31

and dey raise dey sugar, rice, peas, chickens, eggs, cows and just everythin' good to eat.

Every evenin' at three o'clock Old Mistress would call all us litsy
bitsy children in, and we would lay down on pallets and have to go to
sleep. I can hear her now singin' to us pickaninnies. . . .

When I got big 'nough I nursed my mistress's baby. When de baby
go to sleep in de evenin' I would put it in de cradle and lay down by de
cradle and go to sleep. I played a heap when I was little. We played
Susannah Gal, jump rope, callin' cows, runnin', jumpin', skippin', and
just everything we could think of. When I got big enough to cook, I
cooked for dem.

De kitchen of de big house was built way off from de house, and we
cooked on a great big old fireplace. We had swing pots and would
swing dem over de fire and cook and had a big old skillet with legs on
it. We called it an oven and cooked bread and cakes in it.

We had de best mistress and master in de world, and dey was
Christian folks and dey taught us to be Christianlike too. Every Sunday
mornin' Old Master would have all us niggers to de house while he
would sing and pray and read de Bible to us all. Old Master taught us
not to be bad; he taught us to be good. He told us to never steal nor to
tell false tales and not to do anything dat was bad. He said: "You will
reap what you sow; dat you sow it single and reap double." I learned dat
when I was a little child and I ain't forgot it yet. When I got grown I
went de Baptist way. God called my pa to preach, and Old Master let
him preach in de kitchen and in de back yard under de trees. On
preachin' day Old Master took his whole family and all de slaves to
church with him.

Down in de quarters every black family had a one- or two-room log
cabin. We didn't have no floors in dem cabins. Nice dirt floors was de
style den, and we used sage brooms. Took a string and tied de sage
together and had a nice broom out of dat. We would gather broom sage
for our winter brooms just like we gathered our other winter stuff. We
kept our dirt floors swept clean and white. And our bed was big and tall
and had little beds to push under dere. Dey was all little enough to go
under de other, and in de daytime we would push dem all under de big
one and make heaps of room. Our beds were stuffed with hay and straw
and shucks, and, believe me child, dey sure slept good.

When de boys would start to de quarters from de field dey would get
a turn of lidder knots. I expects you knows dem as pine knots. Dat was
what we use for light. When our fire went out we had no fire. Didn't
know nothin' 'bout no matches. To start a fire we would take a skillet
lid and a piece of cotton and a flint rock. Lay cotton on de skillet lid
and take a piece of iron and beat de flint rock till de fire would come.

Sometime we would beat for thirty minutes before de fire would come and start de cotton. Den we would light our pine.

Up at de big house we didn't use lidder knots but used tallow candles for lights. We made de candles from tallow dat we took from cows. We had molds and would put string in dere and leave de end stickin' out to light and melt de tallow and pour it down around de string in de mold.

We used to play at night by moonlight, and I can recollect singin' with de fiddle. Oh, Lord, dat fiddle could almost talk, and I can hear it ringing' now. Sometime we would dance in de moonlight too.

Old Master raised lots of cotton, and women folks carded and spun and wove cloth, den dey dyed it and made clothes. And we knit all de stockings we wore. Dey made dere dye too, from different kinds of bark and leaves and things. Dey would take de bark and boil it and strain it up and let it stand a day, den wet de material in cold water and shake it out and drop in de boilin' dye and let it set 'bout twenty minutes, den take it out and hang it up and let it dry right out of dat dye. Den rinse it in cold water and let it dry. Den it would be ready to make.

I'll tell you how to dye. A little beech bark dyes slate color set with copperas. Hickory bark and bay leaves dye yellow set with chamber lye; bamboo dyes turkey red, set color with copperas. Pine straw dyes purple, set color with chamber lye. To dye cloth brown we would take de cloth and put it in de water where leather had been tanned and let it soak, den set de color with apple vinegar. And we dyed blue with indigo and set de color with alum.

We wore drawers made out of domestic dat come down longer dan our dresses and we wore seven petticoats in de winter with sleeves in dem, and de boys wore old long shirts. Dey didn't know nothin' 'bout no britches till dey was great big, just went round in dey shirttails. And we all wore shoes cause my pa made shoes.

Master taught Pa to make shoes, and de way he done, dey killed a cow and took de hide and tanned it. De way dey tanned it was to take red oak bark and put it in vats made somethin' like troughs dat held water. First he would put in a layer of leather and a layer of oak ashes and a layer of leather and a layer of oak ashes till he got it all in and covered with water. After dat he let it soak till de hair come off de hide. Den he would take de hide out, and it was ready for tannin'. Den de hide was put to soak in with de red oak bark. It stayed in de water till de hide turned tan. Den Pa took de hide out of de red oak dye, and it was a pretty tan. It didn't have to soak long. Den he would get his pattern and cut and make tan shoes out of de tanned hides. We called dem brogans.

Dey planted indigo and it growed just like wheat. When it got ripe dey gathered it, and we would put it in a barrel and let it soak 'bout a week. Den we would take de indigo stems out and squeeze all de juice out of dem and put de juice back in de barrel and let it stand 'bout another week. Den we just stirred and stirred one whole day. We let it set three or four days and den drained de water off and left de settlings and de settlings was bluin' just like we have dese days. We cut ours in little blocks and we dyed clothes with it too.

We made vinegar out of apples. Took overripe apples and ground dem up and put dem in a sack and let it drip. Didn't add no water, and when it got through drippin' we let it sour and strained it and let it stand for six months and had some of de best vinegar ever made.

We had homemade tubs and didn't have no washboards. We had a block and a battlin' stick. We put our clothes in soak, den took dem out of soak and lay dem on de block and take de battlin' stick and battle de dirt out of dem. We mostly used rattan vines for clotheslines, and dey made de best clotheslines dey was.

Old Master raised big patches of tobacco, and when dey gather it dey let it dry and den put it in molasses. After de molasses dripped off, den dey roll it up and twisted it and let it dry in de sun ten or twelve days. It sure was ready for chewin', and it was sweet and stuck together so you could chaw and spit and enjoy it.

De way we got our perfume, we took rose leaves, cape jasmines, and sweet basil and laid dem with our clothes and let dem stay three or four days. Den we had good smellin' clothes dat would last too.

When dere was distressful news Master would ring de bell. When de niggers in de field would hear de bell, everyone would listen and wonder what de trouble was. You'd see dem stirrin' too. Dey would always ring de bell at twelve o'clock. Sometimes dey would think it was somethin' serious, and dey would stand up straight, but if dey could see dey shadow right under dem dey would know it was time for dinner.

De reason so many white folks was rich was dey made money and didn't have nothin' to do but save it. Dey made money and raised everythin' dey used, and just didn't have no use for money. Didn't have no banks in dem days, and Master buried his money.

De floors in de big house was so pretty and white. We always kept dem scoured good. We didn't know what it was to use soap. We just took oak ashes out of de fireplace and sprinkled dem on de floor and scoured with a corn-shuck mop. Den we would sweep de ashes off and rinse two times and let it dry. When it dried it was de cleanest floor dey was. To make it white, clean sand was sprinkled on de floor, and we let it stay a couple of days. Den de floor would be too clean to walk on. De way we dried de floor was with a sack and a rag. We would get down on our knees and dry it so dry.

I remember one night one of Old Master's girls was goin' to get married. Dat was after I was big enough to cook, and we was sure doin' some cookin'. Some of de niggers on de place just naturally would steal, so we cook a big cake of corn bread and iced it all pretty and put it out to cool, and some of dem stole it. Dis way Old Master found out who was doin' de stealin', 'cause it was such a joke on dem dey had to tell.

All Old Master's niggers was married by de white preacher, but he had a neighbor who would marry his niggers hisself. He would say to de man: "Do you want this woman?" and to de girl: "Do you want this boy?" Den he would call de Old Mistress to fetch de broom, and Old Master would hold one end and Old Mistress de other and tell de boy and girl to jump this broom, and he would say: "Dat's your wife." Dey called marryin' like dat "jumpin' de broom."

I can't remember everything I done in dem days, but we didn't have to worry 'bout nothin'. Old Mistress was de one to worry. 'Twasn't den like it is now, no 'twasn't. We had such a good time, and everybody cried when de Yankees cried out: "Free." Other niggers say dey had a hard time before dey was free, but 'twas den like 'tis now. If you had a hard time, we done it ourselves.

Old Master didn't want to part with his niggers, and de niggers didn't want to part with Old Master, so dey thought by comin' to Arkansas dey could have a chance to keep dem. So dey got on dere way. We loaded up our wagons and put up our wagon sheet, and we had plenty to eat and plenty of horse feed. We traveled 'bout fifteen or twenty miles a day and would stop and camp at night. We would cook enough in de mornin' to last all day. De cows was drove together. Some was gentle and some was not, and did dey have a time. I mean, dey *had* a time. While we was on our way Old Master died, and three of de slaves died too. We buried de slaves dere, but we camped while Old Master was carried back to North Carolina. When Old Mistress come back we started on to Arkansas and reached dere safe, but when we got here we found freedom here too. Old Mistress begged us to stay with her, and we stayed till she died. Den dey took her back to Carolina. Dere wasn't nobody left but Miss Nancy, and she soon married and left and I lost track of her and Mr. Tom.

MRS. M. S. FAYMAN

Interviewed at Baltimore, Maryland
Interviewed by ____ Rogers
Age when interviewed: 87

I WAS born in St. Nazaire Parish in Louisiana, about sixty miles south of Baton Rouge, in 1850. My father and mother were Creoles; both of them were people of wealth and prestige in their days and considered very influential. My father's name was Henri de Sales and mother's maiden name was Marguerite Sanchez de Haryne. I had two brothers, Henri and Jackson, named after General Jackson, both of whom died quite young, leaving me the only living child. Both Mother and Father were born and reared in Louisiana. We lived in a large and spacious house surrounded by flowers and situated on a farm containing about seven hundred and fifty acres, on which we raised pelicans for sale in the market at New Orleans.

When I was about five years old I was sent to a private school in Baton Rouge, conducted by French Sisters, where I stayed until I was kidnapped in 1860. At that time I did not know how to speak English. French was the language spoken in my household and by people in the parish.

Baton Rouge, situated on the Mississippi, was a river port and stopping place for all large river boats, especially between New Orleans and large towns and cities north. We children were taken out by the Sisters after school and on Saturdays and holidays to walk. One of the places we went was the wharf. One day in June and a Saturday a large boat was at the wharf going north on the Mississippi River. We children were there. Somehow, I was separated from the other children. I was taken bodily up by a white man, carried on the boat, put in a cabin, and kept there until we got to Louisville, Kentucky, where I was taken off.

After I arrived in Louisville I was taken to a farm near Frankfort and installed there virtually a slave until 1864, when I escaped through the kindness of a delightful Episcopalian woman from Cincinnati, Ohio. As I could not speak English, my chores were to act as tutor and companion for the children of Pierce Buckran Haynes, a well-known slave trader and plantation owner in Kentucky. Haynes wanted his children to speak French and it was my duty to teach them. I was the private companion of three girls and one small boy; each day I had to talk French and write French for them. They became very proficient in French and I in the rudiments of the English language.

I slept in the children's quarters with the Haynes children, ate and played with them. I had all the privileges of the household accorded to me with the exception of one—I never was taken off nor permitted to leave the plantation. While on the plantation I wore good clothes, similar to those of the white children. Haynes was a merciless brutal tyrant with his slaves, punishing them severely and cruelly both by the lash and in the jail on the plantation.

The name of the plantation where I was held as a slave was called Beatrice Manor, after the wife of Haynes. It contained eight thousand acres, of which more than six thousand acres were under cultivation, and having three hundred and fifty colored slaves and five or six overseers, all of whom were white. The overseers were the overlords of the manor, as Haynes dealt extensively in tobacco and trading in slaves and he was away from the plantation nearly all the time. There was located on the top of the large tobacco warehouse a large bell, which was rung at sunup, twelve o'clock, and at sundown, the year round. On the farm the slaves were assigned a task to do each day, and in the event it was not finished they were severely whipped. While I never saw a slave whipped, I did see them afterwards. They were very badly marked and striped by the overseers who did the whipping.

I have been back to the farm on several occasions, the first time in 1872 when I took my father there to show him the farm. At that time it was owned by Colonel Hawkins, a Confederate Army officer. Let me describe the huts. These buildings were built of stone, each one about twenty feet high, fifty feet long, nine feet high in the rear, and about twelve feet high in front, with a slanting roof of chestnut boards and with a sliding door, two windows between each door back and front about two by four feet, at each end a door and window similar to those on the side. There were ten such buildings. Connected to each building there was another building twelve by fifteen feet. This was where the cooking was done. At each end of each building there was a fireplace, built and used for heating purposes. In front of each building there were barrels filled with water supplied by pipes from a large spring, situated about three hundred yards on the side of a hill which was very rocky, where the stones were quarried to build the buildings on the farm. On the outside near each window and door there were iron rings firmly attached to the walls, through which an iron rod was inserted and locked each and every night, making it impossible for those inside to escape.

There was one building used as a jail, built of stone about twenty by forty feet with a hip roof about twenty-five feet high, two-story. On the ground in each end was a fireplace; in one end a small room where the whipping was done. To reach the second story there was built, on the outside, steps leading to a door, through which the female prisoners were taken to the room. All of the buildings had dirt floors.

I do not know much about the Negroes on the plantation who were there at the time. Slaves were brought and taken away always chained together, men walking and women in ox carts. I had heard of several escapes and many were captured. One of the overseers had a pack of six or eight trained bloodhounds which were used to trace escaping slaves.

Before I close let me give you a sketch of my family tree. My grandmother was a Haitian Negress, grandfather a Frenchman, father was a Creole. After returning home in 1864, I completed my high school education in New Orleans in 1870, graduated from Fisk University in 1874, taught French there until 1883, married Professor Fayman, teacher of history and English. Since then I have lived in Washington, New York, and Louisiana.

JOHN FINNELY

Interviewed at Forth Worth, Texas
Interviewer not identified
Age when interviewed: 86

ALABAMA AM de state where I'se born and dat eighty-six year ago, in Jackson County, on Massa Martin Finnely's plantation, and him owns about seventy-five other slaves besides Mammy and me. My pappy am on dat plantation but I don't know him, 'cause Mammy never talks about him except to say, "He am here."

Massa run de cotton plantation but raises stock and feed and corn and cane and rations for de humans such as us. It am different when I'se a youngun dan now. Den, it am needful for to raise everything you need 'cause dey couldn't depend on factory-made goods. Dey could buy shoes and clothes and such, but we'uns could make dem so much cheaper. We'uns make shoes, and leather and clothes and cloth and grinds de meal. And we'uns cures de meat, preserves de fruit, and make 'lasses and brown sugar. All de harness for de mules and de hosses is made and de carts for haulin'. Massa make peach brandy and him have he own still.

De work am 'vided 'twist de cullud folks and us always have certain duties to do. I'se am de field hand and before I'se old enough for to do dat, dey has me help with de chores and errands.

Us have de cabins of logs with one room and one door and one window hole, and bunks for sleepin'. But no cookin' am done here. It am done in de cookhouse by de cooks for all us niggers and we'uns eats in de eatin' shed. De rations am good, plain victuals, and dere plenty of it, and about twice a week dere somethin' for treat. Massa sure am particular about feedin', specially for de younguns in de nursery. You see, dere am de nursery for such what needs care while dere mammies am a-workin'.

Massa feed plenty and him demand plenty work. Dat cause heap of trouble on dat plantation, 'cause whippin's am given and hard ones, too. Lots of times at de end of de day I'se so tired I'se couldn't speak for to stop mule, I just have to lean back on de lines.

Dis nigger never gits whipped except for dis, before I'se a field hand. Massa use me for huntin' and use me for de gun rest. When him have de long shot I bends over and puts de hands on de knees and Massa puts his gun on my back for to get de good aim. What him kills I runs and fetches and carries de game for him. I turns de squirrels for him and dat disaway: de squirrel always go to other side from de hunter and I walks around de tree and de squirrel see me and go to Massa's side de tree and he gets shot.

All dat not so bad, but when he shoots de duck in de water and I has to fetch it out, dat give me de worryment. De first time he tells me to go in de pond I'se skeert, powerful skeert. I takes off de shirt and pants but there I stands. I steps in de water, den back again, and again. Massa am gettin' mad. He say, "Swim in dere and get dat duck." "Yes sir, Massa," I says, but I won't go in dat water till Massa hit me some licks. I couldn't never get used to bein' de water dog for de ducks.

De worst whippin' I seed was give to Clarinda. She hits Massa with de hoe 'cause he try 'fere with her and she try stop him. She am put on de log and give five hundred lashes. She am over dat log all day and when dey takes her off, she am limp and act deadlike. For a week she am in de bunk. Dat whippin' cause plenty trouble and dere lots of arguments among de white folks round dere.

We has some joyments on de plantation, no parties or dancin' but we has de corn huskin' and de nigger fights. For de corn huskin' everybody come to one place and dey gives de prize for findin' de red ear. On Massa's place de prize am brandy or you am allowed to kiss de gal you calls for. While us huskin' us sing lots, but, I'se not gwine sing any dem songs, 'cause I'se forget and my voice sound like de bray of de mule.

De nigger fights am more for de white folks' joyment but de slaves am allowed to see it. De massas of plantations match dere niggers 'cording to size, and bet on dem. Massa Finnely have one nigger what weighs about 150 pounds and him powerful good fighter and he like to fight. None lasts long with him. Den a new nigger comes to fight him.

Dat field am held at night by de pine torchlight. A ring am made by de folks standin' around in de circle. Dey's allowed to do anything with dey hands and head and teeth. Nothin' barred except de knife and de club. Dem two niggers gets in de ring and Tom he starts quick, and dat new nigger he starts just as quick. Dat surprise Tom and when dey comes together it like two bulls—kersmash—it sounds like dat. Den it am hit and kick and bite and butt anywhere and any place for to best de other. De one on de bottom bites knees and anything him can do. Dat's de way it go for half de hour.

Findly dat new nigger gets Tom in de stomach with he knee and a lick side de jaw at the same time and down to Tom, and de other nigger jumps on him with both feets, den straddle him and hits with right, left, right, left, right, side Tom's head. Dere Tom lay, makin' no resistance. Everybody am sayin', "Tom have met he match, him am done." Both am bleedin' and am awful sight. Well, dat new nigger relaxes for to get he wind and den Tom, quick like de flash flips him off and jump to he feet and before dat new nigger could get to he feet, Tom kicks him in de stomach, again and again. Dat nigger's body start to quaver and he massa say, "Dat 'nough." Dat de closest Tom ever come to gettin' whipped what I'se know of.

I becomes a runaway nigger short time after dat fight. De War am started den for about a year, or somethin' like dat, and de Federals am north of us. I hears de niggers talk about it, and about runnin' away to freedom. I thinks and thinks about gettin' freedom, and I'se goin' run off. Den I thinks of de patterrollers and what happen if dey cotches me off de place without de pass. Den I thinks of some joyment such as de corn huskin' and de fights and de singin' and I don't know what to do. I tells you one singin' but I can't sing it:

> De moonlight, a shinin' star,
> De big owl hootin' in de tree;
> O, bye, my baby, ain't you gwineter sleep,
> A-rockin' on my knee?

> Bye, my honey baby,
> A-rockin' on my knee,
> Baby done gone to sleep,
> Owl hush hootin' in de tree.

> She gone to sleep, honey baby sleep,
> A-rockin' on my, a-rockin' on my knee.

Now, back to de freedom. One night about ten niggers run away. De next day we'uns hears nothin', so I says to myself, "De patterrollers don't catch dem." Den I makes up my mind to go and I leaves with de chunk of meat and corn bread and am on my way, half skeert to death. I sure has de eyes open and de ears forward, watchin' for de patterrollers. I steps off de road in de night, at sight of anything, and in de day I takes to de woods. It takes me two days to make dat trip and just once de patters pass me by. I am in de thicket watchin' dem and I'se sure dey goin' search dat thicket, 'cause dey stops and am a-talkin' and lookin' my way. Dey stands dere for a li'l bit and den one comes my way. Lawd-a-mighty! dat sure look like de end, but dat man stop and den look and look. Den he pick up somethin' and goes back. It am a bottle and dey all takes de drink and rides on. I'se sure in de sweat and I don't tarry dere long.

De Yanks am camped near Bellfound and dere's where I get to. Imagine my s'prise when I finds all de ten runaway niggers am dere too. Dat am on Sunday. And on de Monday de Yanks puts us on de freight train and we goes to Stevenson, in Alabama. Dere, us put to work buildin' breastworks. But after de few days, I gets sent to de headquarters at Nashville, in Tennessee.

I'se water toter dere for de army and dere am no fightin' at first but before long dey starts de battle. Dat battle am a experience for me. De noise am awful, just one steady roar of guns and de cannons. De window glass in Nashville am all shook out from de shakement of de cannons. Dere dead mens all over de ground and lots of wounded and some cussin' and some prayin'. Some am moanin' and dis and dat one cry for de water and, God-a-mighty I don't want any such again. Dere am men carryin' de dead off de field, but dey can't keep up with de cannons. I helps bury de dead and den I gets sent to Murfreesboro and dere it am just the same.

You knows when Abe Lincoln am shot? Well, I'se in Nashville den and it am near de end of de War and I am standin' on Broadway Street talkin' with de sergeant when a man walks up and him shakes hands with me and says, "I'se proud to meet a brave, young fellow like you." Dat man am Andrew Johnson and him come to be President after Abe's dead.

I stays in Nashville when de War am over and I marries Tennessee House in 1875. She died July 10, 1936. Dat make sixty-one year dat we'uns am together. Her old missy am now livin' in Arlington Heights, right here in Fort Worth and her name am Mallard and she come from Tennessee too.

I comes here from Tennessee fifty-one year ago and at first I farms and den I works for de packin' plants till dey lets me out, 'cause I'se too old for to do 'nough work for dem.

I has eight boys and three girls, dat make eleven children, and dey makin' scatterment all over de country so I'se alone in my old age. I has dat seventeen dollars a month pension what I get from de state.

Dat am de end of de road.

DELIA GARLIC

Interviewed in Montgomery, Alabama
Interviewed by Margaret Fowler
Age when interviewed: 100

SLAVERY DAYS was hell. I was growed up when de War come, and I was a mother before it closed. Babies was snatched from dere mother's breast and sold to speculators. Chillens was separated from sisters and brothers and never saw each other again. 'Course dey cry. You think they not cry when dey was sold like cattle? I could tell you about it all day, but even den you couldn't guess de awfulness of it.

It's bad to belong to folks dat own you soul and body, dat can tie you up to a tree, with yo' face to d' tree and yo' arms fastened tight around it, who take a long curlin' whip and cut de blood every lick. Folks a mile away could hear dem awful whippings. Dey was a terrible part of livin'.

I was born at Powhatan, Virginia, and was the youngest of thirteen chillen. I never seed none of my brothers and sisters 'cept brother William. Him and my mother and me was brought in a speculator's drove to Richmond and put in a warehouse with a drove of other niggers. Den we was all put on a block and sold to de highest bidder. I never seed brother William again.

Mammy and me was sold to a man by the name of Carter, who was de sheriff of de county. Dey wasn't no good times at his house. He was a widower and his daughter kept house for him. I nursed for her and one day I was playin' with de baby. It hurt its li'l hand and commenced to cry, and she whirl on me, pick up a hot iron and run it all down my arm and hand. It took off de flesh when she done it.

After a while, Marster married again, but things weren't no better. I seed his wife blackin' her eyebrows with smut one day, so I thought I'd black mine just for fun. I rubbed some smut on my eyebrows and forgot to rub it off, and she cotched me. She was powerful mad and yelled: "You black devil, I'll show you how to mock your betters." Den she pick up a stick of stovewood and flails it against my head. I didn't know

43

nothin' more till I come to, lyin' on de floor. I heard de mistis say to one of de girls: "I thought her thick skull and cap of wool could take it better than that."

I kept on stayin' dere, and one night de marster come in drunk and set at de table with his head lollin' around. I was waitin' on de table, and he look up and see me. I was scared, and dat made him awful mad. He called an overseer and told him: "Take her out and beat some sense in her."

I begin to cry and run and run in de night, but finally I run back by de quarters and heard Mammy callin' me. I went in, and right away dey come for me. A horse was standin' in front of de house, and I was took dat very night to Richmond and sold to a speculator again. I never seed my mammy anymore.

I has thought many times through all dese years how Mammy looked dat night. She pressed my hand in both of hers and said: "Be good and trust in de Lord." Trustin' was de only hope of de poor black critters in dem days. Us just prayed for strength to endure it to de end. We didn't 'spect nothin' but to stay in bondage till we died.

I was sold by de speculator to a man in McDonough, Georgia. I don't recollect his name, but he was openin' a big hotel at McDonough and bought me to wait on tables. But when de time come around to pay for me, his hotel done fail. Den de Atlanta man dat bought de hotel bought me, too. Before long, though, I was sold to a man by de name of Garlic, down in Louisiana, and I stayed with him till I was freed. I was a regular field hand, plowin' and hoein' and choppin' cotton.

Us heard talk about de War, but us didn't pay no 'tention. Us never dreamed dat freedom would ever come.

Us didn't have no parties on our plantation; nothin' like dat. Us didn't have no clothes for goin' round. I never had a undershirt until just before my first child was borned. I never had nothin' but a shimmy and a slip for a dress, and it was made outen de cheapest cloth dat could be bought, unbleached cloth, coarse, but made to last.

Us didn't know nothin' 'cept to work. Us was up by three or four in de mornin' and everybody got dey somethin' to eat in de kitchen. Dey didn't give us no way to cook, nor nothin' to cook in our cabins. Soon as us dressed us went by de kitchen and got our piece of corn bread. Dey wasn't even no salt in dem last years. Dat piece of corn bread was all us had for breakfast, and for supper us had de same. For dinner us had boiled victuals; greens, peas, and sometimes beans. Us never knowed nothin' about coffee.

One mornin' I 'members I had started to de field, and on de way I lost my piece of bread. I didn't know what to do. I started back to try to find it, and it was too dark to see. But I walk right slow, and had a dog dat walked with me. He went on ahead, and after a while I come on him lyin' dere guardin' dat piece of bread. He never touched it, so I gived him some of it.

Just before de War I married a man named Chatfield from another plantation; but he was took off to war and I never seed him again. After a while I married a boy on de plantation named Miles Garlic.

Massa Garlic had two boys in de War. When dey went off de massa and mistis cried, but it made us glad to see dem cry. Dey made us cry so much.

When we knowed we was free, everybody wanted to get out. De rule was dat if you stayed in yo' cabin you could keep it, but if you left, you lost it. Miles was workin' at Wetumpka, and he slipped in and out so us could keep on livin' in de cabin. My second baby soon come, and right den I made up my mind to go to Wetumpka where Miles was workin' for de railroad. I went on down dere and us settled down.

After Miles died, I lived dere long as I could and den come to Montgomery to live with my son. I'se eatin' white bread now and havin' de best time of my life. But when de Lord say, "Delia, well done; come up higher," I'll be glad to go.

ROBERT GLENN

Interviewed at Raleigh, North Carolina
Interviewed by Pat Matthews
Age when interviewed: 87

I WAS a slave before and during the Civil War. I am eighty-seven years old. I was born September 16, 1850. I was born in Orange County, North Carolina, near Hillsboro. At that time Durham was just a platform at the station and no house there whatever. The platform was lighted with a contraption shaped like a basket and burning coal that gave off a blaze. There were holes in this metal basket for the cinders to fall through.

I belonged to a man named Bob Hall; he was a widower. He had three sons, Thomas, Nelson, and Lambert. He died when I was eight years old and I was put on the block and sold in Nelson Hall's yard by the son of Bob Hall. I saw my brother and sister sold on this same plantation. My mother belonged to the Halls, and father belonged to the Glenns. They sold me away from my father and mother and I was carried to the state of Kentucky. I was bought by a Negro speculator by the name of Henry Long, who lived not far from Hurdles Mill in Person County. I was not allowed to tell my mother and father good-bye. I was bought and sold three times in one day.

My father's time was hired out and, as he knew a trade, he had by working overtime saved up a considerable amount of money. After the speculator, Henry Long, bought me, Mother went to Father and pled with him to buy me from him and let the white folks hire me out. No slave could own a slave. Father got the consent and help of his owners to buy me and they asked Long to put me on the block again. Long did so and named his price but when he learned who had bid me off, he backed down. Later in the day he put me on the block and named another price much higher than the price formerly set. He was asked by the white folks to name his price for his bargain and he did so. I was again put on the auction block and Father bought me in, putting up the cash. Long then flew into a rage and cursed my father saying, "You

46

damn black son of a bitch, you think you are white do you? Now just to show you you are black, I will not let you have your son at any price."

Father knew it was all off. Mother was frantic, but there was nothing they could do about it. They had to stand and see the speculator put me on his horse behind him and ride away without allowing either of them to tell me good-bye. I figure I was sold three times in one day, as the price asked was offered in each instance. Mother was told under threat of a whipping not to make any outcry when I was carried away.

He took me to his home, but on the way he stopped for refreshments, at a plantation, and while he was eating and drinking, he put me into a room where two white women were spinning flax. I was given a seat across the room from where they were working. After I had sat there awhile wondering where I was going and thinking about Mother and home, I went to one of the women and asked, "Missus, when will I see my mother again?" She replied, "I don't know, child. Go and sit down." I went back to my seat and as I did so both the women stopped spinning for a moment, looked at each other, and one of them remarked, "Almighty God, this slavery business is a horrible thing. Chances are this boy will never see his mother again." This remark nearly killed me, as I began to fully realize my situation.

Long, the Negro trader, soon came back, put me on his horse and finished the trip to his home. He kept me at his home awhile and then traded me to a man named William Moore who lived in Person County.

Moore at this time was planning to move to Kentucky, which he soon did, taking me with him. My mother found out by the "grapevine telegraph" that I was going to be carried to Kentucky. She got permission and came to see me before they carried me off. When she started home I was allowed to go part of the way with her, but they sent two Negro girls with us to insure my return. We were allowed to talk privately, but while we were doing so, the two girls stood a short distance away and watched, as the marster told them when they left that if I escaped they would be whipped every day until I was caught. When the time of parting came and I had to turn back, I burst out crying loud. I was so weak from sorrow I could not walk, and the two girls who were with me took me by each arm and led me along half carrying me.

This man Moore carried me and several other slaves to Kentucky. We traveled by train by way of Nashville, Tennessee. My thoughts are not familiar with the happenings of this trip but I remember that we walked a long distance at one place on the trip from one depot to another.

We finally reached Kentucky and Moore stopped at his brother's plantation until he could buy one; then we moved on it. My marster was named William Moore and my missus was named Martha Whitfield Moore. It was a big plantation and he hired a lot of help and had white tenants besides the land he worked with slaves. There were only six slaves used as regular field hands during his first year in Kentucky.

The food was generally common. Hog meat and corn bread most all the time. Slaves got biscuits only on Sunday morning. Our clothes were poor and I worked barefooted most of the time, winter and summer. No books, papers, or anything concerning education was allowed the slaves by his rules and the customs of these times.

Marster Moore had four children, among whom was one boy about my age. The girls were named Atona, Beulah, and Minnie, and the boy was named Crosby. He was mighty brilliant. We played together. He was the only white boy there, and he took a great liking to me, and we loved each other devotedly. Once in a undertone he asked me how I would like to have an education. I was overjoyed at the suggestion and he at once began to teach me secretly. I studied hard and he soon had me so I could read and write well. I continued studying and he continued teaching me. He furnished me books and slipped all the papers he could get to me and I was the best educated Negro in the community without anyone except the slaves knowing what was going on.

All the slaves on Marster's plantation lived the first year we spent in Kentucky in a one-room house with one fireplace. There was a dozen or more who all lived in this one-room house. Marster built himself a large house having seven rooms. He worked his slaves himself and never had any overseers. We worked from sun to sun in the fields and then worked at the house after getting in from the fields as long as we could see. I have never seen a patterroller, but when I left the plantation in slavery time I got a pass. I have never seen a jail for slaves, but I have seen slaves whipped and I was whipped myself. I was whipped particularly about a saddle I left in the night after using it during the day. My flesh was cut up so bad that the scars are on me to this day.

We were not allowed to have prayer meetings, but we went to the white folks' church to services sometimes. There were no looms, mills, or shops on the plantation at Marster Moore's. I kept the name of Glenn through all the years as Marster Moore did not change his slaves' names to his family name. My mother was named Martha Glenn and Father was named Bob Glenn.

I was in the field when I first heard of the Civil War. The woman who looked after Henry Hall and myself (both slaves) told me she heard Marster say old Abraham Lincoln was tryin' to free the niggers. Marster finally pulled me up and went and joined the Confederate Army. Kentucky split and part joined the North and part the South.

The war news kept slipping through of success for first one side, then the other. Sometimes Marster would come home, spend a few days, and then go again to the War. It seemed he influenced a lot of men to join the Southern army, among them was a man named Enoch Moorehead. Moorehead was killed in a few days after he joined the Southern army.

Marster Moore fell out with a lot of his associates in the army and some of them who were from the same community became his bitter enemies. Tom Foushee was one of them. Marster became so alarmed over the threats on his life made by Foushee and others that he was afraid to stay in his own home at night, and he built a little camp one and one-half miles from his home and he and Missus spent their nights there on his visits home. Foushee finally came to the Great House one night heavily armed. Came right on into the house and inquired for Marster. We told him Marster was away. Foushee lay down on the floor and waited a long time for him. Marster was at the little camp but we would not tell where he was.

Foushee left after spending most of the night at Marster's. As he went out into the yard, when leaving, Marster's bulldog growled at him and he shot him dead.

Marster went to Henderson, Kentucky, the county seat of Henderson County, and surrendered to the Federal army and took the Oath of Allegiance. Up to that time I had seen a few Yankees. They stopped now and then at Marster's and got their breakfast. They always asked about buttermilk, they seemed to be very fond of it. They were also fond of ham. But we had the ham meat buried in the ground. This was about the close of the War. A big army of Yankees came through a few months later and soon we heard of the surrender. A few days after this, Marster told me to catch two horses, that we had to go to Dickenson, which was the county seat of Webster County. On the way to Dickenson he said to me, "Bob, did you know you are free and Lincoln has freed you? You are as free as I am." We went to the Freedman's Bureau and went into the office. A Yankee officer looked me over and asked Marster my name, and informed me I was free, and asked me whether or not I wanted to keep living with Moore. I did not know what to do, so I told him yes. A fixed price of seventy-five dollars and board was then set as the salary I should receive per year for my work. The Yankee told me to let him know if I was not paid as agreed.

I went back home and stayed a year. During the year I hunted a lot at night and thoroughly enjoyed being free. I took my freedom by degrees and remained obedient and respectful, but still wondering and thinking of what the future held for me. After I retired at night I made plan after plan and built air castles as to what I would do. At this time

I formed a great attachment for the white man, Mr. Atlas Chandler, with whom I hunted. He bought my part of the game we caught and favored me in other ways. Mr. Chandler had a friend, Mr. Dewitt Yarborough, who was an adventurer and trader, and half brother to my ex-marster, Mr. Moore, with whom I was then staying. He is responsible for me taking myself into my own hands and getting out of feeling I was still under obligations to ask my marster or missus when I desired to leave the premises. Mr. Yarborough's son was off at school at a place called Kiloh, Kentucky, and he wanted to carry a horse to him and also take along some other animals for trading purposes. He offered me a new pair of pants to make the trip for him and I accepted the job. I delivered the horse to his son and started for home. On the way back I ran into Uncle Squire Yarborough who once belonged to Dewitt Yarborough. He persuaded me to go home with him to a wedding in Union County, Kentucky. The wedding was twenty miles away and we walked the entire distance. It was a double wedding, two couples were married. Georgianna Hawkins was married to George Ross and Steve Carter married a woman whose name I do not remember. This was in the winter during the Christmas holidays and I stayed in the community until about the first of January, then I went back home. I had been thinking for several days before I went back home as to just what I must tell Mr. Moore and as to how he felt about the matter, and what I would get when I got home. In my dilemma I almost forgot I was free.

I got home at night and my mind and heart was full but I was surprised at the way he treated me. He acted kind and asked me if I was going to stay with him next year. I was pleased. I told him, "Yes sir!" and then I lay down and went to sleep. He had a boss man on his plantation then and next morning he called me, but I just couldn't wake. I seemed to be in a trance or something, I had recently lost so much sleep. He called me the second time and still I did not get up. Then he came in and spanked my head. I jumped up and went to work feeding the stock and splitting wood for the day's cooking and fires. I then went in and ate my breakfast. Mr. Moore told me to hitch a team of horses to a wagon and go to a neighbor's five miles away for a load of hogs. I refused to do so. They called me into the house and asked me what I was doing about it. I said I do not know. As I said that I stepped out of the door and left.

I went straight to the county seat and hired to Dr. George Rasby in Webster County for one hundred dollars per year. I stayed there one year. I got uneasy in Kentucky. The whites treated the blacks awful bad so I decided to go to Illinois, as I thought a Negro might have a better chance there, it being a Northern state. I was kindly treated and soon began to save money, but all through the years there was a thought that haunted me in my dreams and in my waking hours, and this thought was of my mother, whom I had not seen or heard of in many years.

Finally one cold morning in early December I made a vow that I was going to North Carolina and see my mother if she was still living. I had plenty of money for the trip. I wrote the postmaster in Roxboro, North Carolina, asking him to inform my mother I was still living, and telling him the circumstances, mailing a letter at the same time telling her I was still alive but saying nothing of my intended visit to her. I left Illinois bound for North Carolina on December fifteenth and in a few days I was at my mother's home. I tried to fool them. There were two men with me and they called me by a fictitious name, but when I shook my mother's hand I held it a little too long and she suspicioned something. Still she held herself until she was more sure. When she got a chance she came to me and said, "Ain't you my child? Tell me ain't you my child whom I left on the road near Mr. Moore's before the War?"

I broke down and began to cry. Mother and Father did not know me, but Mother suspicioned I was her child. Father had a few days previously remarked that he did not want to die without seeing his son once more. I could not find language to express my feelings. I did not know before I came home whether my parents were dead or alive. This Christmas I spent in the county and state of my birth and childhood with Mother, Father, and freedom was the happiest period of my entire life, because those who were torn apart in bondage and sorrow several years previous were now united in freedom and happiness.

ANDREW GOODMAN

Interviewed at Dallas, Texas
Interviewer not identified
Age when interviewed: 97

I WAS born in slavery and I think them days was better for the niggers than the days we see now. One thing was, I never was cold and hungry when my old master lived, and I has been plenty hungry and cold a lot of times since he is gone. But sometimes I think Marse Goodman was the bestest man God made in a long time.

My mother, Martha Goodman, belonged to Marse Bob Goodman when she was born, but my paw come from Tennessee and Marse Bob heired him from some of his kinfolks what died over there. The Goodmans must have been fine folks all-a-way round, 'cause my paw said them that raised him was good to they niggers. Old Marse never 'lowed none of his nigger families separated. He 'lowed he thought it right and fittin' that folks stay together, though I heard tell of some that didn't think so.

My missus was just as good as Marse Bob. My maw was a puny little woman that wasn't able to do work in the fields, and she puttered round the house for the Missus, doin' little odd jobs. I played round with little Miss Sallie and little Mr. Bob, and I ate with them and slept with them. I used to sweep off the steps and do things, and she'd brag on me. Many is the time I'd get to noddin' and go to sleep, and she'd pick me up and put me in bed with her chillen.

Marse Bob didn't put his little niggers in the fields till they's big 'nough to work, and the mammies was give time off from the fields to come back to the nursin' home to suck the babies. He didn't never put the niggers out in bad weather. He give us somethin' to do, in out of the weather, like shellin' corn, and the women could spin and knit. They made us plenty of good clothes. In summer we wore long shirts, split up the sides, made out of lowerings—that's same as cotton sacks was made out of. In winter we had good jeans and knitted sweaters and knitted socks.

My paw was a shoemaker. He'd take a calfhide and make shoes with the hairy sides turned in, and they was warm and kept your feet dry. My maw spent a lot of time cardin' and spinnin' wool, and I always had plenty things.

Life was purty fine with Marse Bob. He was a man of plenty. He had a lot of land and he built him a log house when he come to Texas. He had several hundred head of cattle and more than that many hogs. We raised cotton and grain and chickens and vegetables and most anything anybody could ask for.

Some places the masters give out a peck of meal and so many pounds of meat to a family for them a week's rations, and if they et it up that was all they got. But Marse Bob always give out plenty and said, "If you need more, you can have it, 'cause ain't any going to suffer on my place."

He built us a church, and a old man, Kenneth Lyons, who was a slave of the Lyons family nearby, used to get a pass every Sunday mornin' and come preach to us. He was a man of good learnin' and the best preacher I ever heard. He baptized in a little old mudhole down back of our place. Nearly all the boys and gals gets converted when they's about twelve or fifteen year old. Then on Sunday afternoon, Marse Bob learned us to read and write. He told us we oughta get all the learnin' we could.

Once a week the slaves could have any night they want for a dance or frolic. Mance McQueen was a slave belonging on the Dewberry place what could play a fiddle, and his master give him a pass to come play for us. Marse Bob give us chickens or kilt a fresh beef or let us make 'lasses candy. We could choose any night, 'cept in the fall of the year. Then we worked awful hard and didn't have the time. We had a gin run by horsepower and after sundown, when we left the fields, we used to gin a bale of cotton every night. Marse always give us from Christmas Eve through New Year's Day off, to make up for the hard work in the fall.

Christmas time everybody got a present and Marse Bob give a big hog to every four families. We had money to buy whiskey with. In spare time we'd make corn-shuck horse collars and all kinds of baskets, and Marse bought them off us. What he couldn't use, he sold for us. We'd take post oak and split it thin with drawin' knives and let it get tough in the sun, and then weave it into cotton baskets and fish baskets and little fancy baskets. The men spent they money on whiskey, 'cause everything else was furnished. We raised our own tobacco and hung it in the barn to season, and anybody could go get it when they wanted it. We always got Saturday afternoons off to fish and hunt. We used to have fish fries and plenty of game in dem days.

Course, we used to hear about other places where they had nigger drivers and beat the slaves. But I never did see or hear tell of one of master's slaves gettin' a beatin'. We had a overseer, but didn't know what a nigger driver was. Marse Bob had some nigger dogs like other places and used to train them for fun. He'd get some of the boys to run for a hour or so and then put the dogs on the trail. He'd say, "If you hear them gettin' near, take to a tree." But Marse Bob never had no niggers to run off.

Old man Briscoll, who had a place next to ours, was vicious cruel. He was mean to his own blood, beatin' his chillen. His slaves was a-feared all the time and hated him. Old Charlie, a good old man who belonged to him, run away and stayed six months in the woods before Briscoll cotched him. The niggers used to help feed him, but one day a nigger 'trayed him and Briscoll put the dogs on him and cotched him. He made to Charlie like he wasn't goin' to hurt him none and got him to come peaceful. When he took him home, he tied him and beat him for a terrible long time. Then he took a big, pine torch and let burnin' pitch drop in spots all over him. Old Charlie was sick about four months and then he died.

Marse Bob knowed me better'n most the slaves, 'cause I was round the house more. One day he called all the slaves to the yard. He only had sixty-six then, 'cause he 'vided with his son and daughter when they married. He made a little speech. He said, "I'm going to a war, but I don't think I'll be gone long, and I'm turning the overseer off and leaving Andrew in charge of the place, and I wants everything to go on, just like I was here. Now, you all mind what Andrew says, 'cause if you don't, I'll make it rough on you when I come back home." He was joking, though, 'cause he wouldn't have done nothing to them.

Then he said to me, "Andrew, you is old 'nough to be a man and look after things. Take care of Missus and see that none of the niggers wants, and try to keep the place going."

We didn't know what the War was about, but Master was gone four years. When Old Missus heard from him, she'd call all the slaves and tell us the news and read us his letters. Little parts of it she wouldn't read. We never heard of him getting hurt none, but if he had, Old Missus wouldn't tell us, 'cause the niggers used to cry and pray over him all the time. We never heard tell what the War was about.

When Marse Bob come home, he sent for all the slaves. He was sitting in a yard chair, all tuckered out, and shook hands all round, and said he's glad to see us. Then he said, "I got something to tell you. You is just as free as I is. You don't belong to nobody but yourselves. We went to the War and fought, but the Yankees done whip us, and they say the niggers is free. You can go where you wants to go, or you can stay here, just as you likes." He couldn't help but cry.

The niggers cry and don't know much what Marse Bob means. They is sorry about the freedom, 'cause they don't know where to go, and they's always 'pend on Old Marse to look after them. Three families went to get farms for theyselves, but the rest just stay on for hands on the old place.

The Federals has been coming by, even before Old Marse come home. They all come by, carrying they little budgets and if they was walking they'd look in the stables for a horse or mule, and they just took what they wanted of corn or livestock. They done the same after Marse Bob come home. He just said, "Let them go they way, 'cause that's what they're going to do, anyway." We was scareder of them than we was of the devil. But they spoke right kindly of us colored folks. They said, "If you got a good master and want to stay, well, you can do that, but now you can go where you want to, 'cause ain't nobody going to stop you."

The niggers can't hardly get used to the idea. When they wants to leave the place, they still go up to the Big House for a pass. They just can't understand about the freedom. Old Marse or Missus say, "You don't need no pass. All you got to do is just take your foot in your hand and go."

It seem like the War just plumb broke Old Marse up. It wasn't long till he moved into Tyler and left my paw running the farm on a half-ance with him and the nigger workers. He didn't live long, but I forgets just how long. But when Mr. Bob heired the old place, he 'lowed we'd just go 'long the way his paw has made the trade with my paw.

Young Mr. Bob apparently done the first rascality I ever heard of a Goodman doing. The first year we worked for him we raised lots of grain and other things and fifty-seven bales of cotton. Cotton was fifty-two cents a pound, and he shipped it all away, but all he ever gave us was a box of candy and a sack of store tobacco and a sack of sugar. He said the 'signment done got lost. Paw said to let it go, 'cause we had always lived by what the Goodmans had said.

I got married and lived on the old place till I was in my late fifties. I had seven chillen, but if I got any livin' now, I don't know where they is. My paw and maw got to own a little piece of land not far from the old place, and paw lived to be 102 and maw 106. I'm the last one of any of my folks.

ARNOLD GRAGSTON

Interviewed in Jacksonville, Florida
Interviewed by Martin Richardson
Age when interviewed: 97

MOST OF the slaves didn't know when they was born, but I did. You see, I was born on a Christmas mornin'—it was in 1840. I was a full-grown man when I finally got my freedom.

Before I got it, though, I helped a lot of others get theirs—Lord only knows how many; might have been as much as two, three hundred. It was way more than a hundred, I know. But that all came after I was a young man—"grown" enough to know a pretty girl when I saw one, and to go chasing after her, too.

I was born on a plantation that belonged to Mr. Jack Tabb, in Mason County, just across the river, in Kentucky. Mr. Tabb was a pretty good man. He used to beat us, sure, but not nearly so much as others did, some of his own kin people, even. But he was kinda funny sometimes; he used to have a special slave who didn't have nothin' to do but teach the rest of us—we had about ten on the plantation and a lot on the other plantations near us—how to read and write and figger. Mr. Tabb liked us to know how to figger. But sometimes, when he would send for us and we would be a long time comin', he would ask us where we had been. If we told him we had been learnin' to read, he would near beat the daylights out of us—after gettin' somebody to teach us. I think he did some of that so that the other owners wouldn't say he was spoilin' his slaves.

He was funny about us marryin', too. He would let us go a-courtin' on the other plantations near anytime we liked, if we were good. And if we found somebody we wanted to marry, and she was on a plantation that belonged to one of his kinfolks or to a friend, he would swap a slave so that the husband and wife could be together. Sometimes, when he couldn't do this, he would let a slave work all day on his plantation and live with his wife at night on her plantation. Some of the other owners was always talkin' about his spoilin' us.

He wasn't a Democrat like the rest of 'em in the county. He belonged to the Know Nothin' Party, and he was a real leader in it. He used to always be makin' speeches, and sometimes his best friends wouldn't be speaking to him for days at a time.

Mr. Tabb was always specially good to me. He used to let me go all about—I guess he had to—couldn't get too much work out of me, even when he kept me right under his eyes. I learned fast, too, and I think he kinda liked that. He used to call Sandy Davis, the slave who taught me, "the smartest nigger in Kentucky."

It was 'cause he used to let me go around in the day and night so much that I came to be the one who carried the runnin'-away slaves over the river. It was funny the way I started it, too.

I didn't have no idea of ever gettin' mixed up in any sort of business like that, until one special night. I hadn't even thought of rowing across the river myself. But one night I had gone on another plantation courtin', and the old woman whose house I went to told me she had a real pretty girl there who wanted to go across the river, and would I take her? I was scared and backed out in a hurry. But then I saw the girl, and she was such a pretty little thing—brown-skinned and kinda rosy, and looking as scared as I was feelin'—so it wasn't long before I was listenin' to the old woman tell me when to take her and where to leave her on the other side.

I didn't have nerve enough to do it that night, though, and I told them to wait for me until tomorrow night. All the next day I kept seeing Mr. Tabb laying a rawhide across my back or shootin' me, and kept seeing that scared little brown girl back at the house, looking at me with her big eyes and askin' me if I wouldn't just row her across to Ripley, [Ohio]. Me and Mr. Tabb lost, and soon as dusk settled that night, I was at the old lady's house.

I don't know how I ever rowed that boat across the river. The current was strong and I was trembling. I couldn't see a thing there in the dark, but I felt that girl's eyes. We didn't dare to whisper, so I couldn't tell her how sure I was that Mr. Tabb or some of the other owners would "tear me up" when they found out what I had done. I just knew they would find out.

I was worried, too, about where to put her out of the boat. I couldn't ride her across the river all night, and I didn't know a thing about the other side. I had heard a lot about it from other slaves, but I thought it was just about like Mason County, with slaves and masters, overseers and rawhides, so I just knew that if I pulled the boat up and went to asking people where to take her I would get a beating or get killed.

I don't know whether it seemed like a long time or a short time, now—it's so long ago. I know it was a long time rowing there in the

cold and worryin', but it was short, too, 'cause as soon as I did get on
the other side the big-eyed, brown-skinned girl would be gone. Well,
pretty soon I saw a tall light, and I remembered what the old lady had
told me about looking for that light and rowing to it. I did, and when I
got up to it, two men reached down and grabbed her. I started tremblin'
all over again and prayin'. Then, one of the men took my arm and I just
felt down inside of me that the Lord had got ready for me. "You hungry, boy?" is what he asked me, and if he hadn't been holdin' me, I
think I would have fell backward into the river.

That was my first trip. It took me a long time to get over my scared
feelin', but I finally did, and I soon found myself goin' back across the
river with two or three people, and sometimes a whole boatload. I got
so I used to make three and four trips a month.

What did my passengers look like? I can't tell you any more about it
than you can, and you wasn't there. After that first girl—no, I never did
see her again—I never saw my passengers. It would have to be the
"black nights" of the moon when I would carry them, and I would meet
them out in the open or in a house without a single light. The only way
I knew who they were was to ask them, "What you say?" And they
would answer, "Menare." I don't know what that word meant—it came
from the Bible. I only know that that was the password I used, and all
of them that I took over told it to me before I took them.

I guess you wonder what I did with them after I got them over the
river. Well, there in Ripley was a man named Mr. Rankins. I think the
rest of his name was John. He had a regular station there on his place
for escaping slaves. You see, Ohio was a free state, and once they got
over the river from Kentucky or Virginia, Mr. Rankins could strut them
all around town, and nobody would bother them. The only reason we
use to land 'em quietly at night was so that whoever brought 'em could
go back for more, and because we had to be careful that none of the
owners had followed us. Every once in a while they would follow a boat
and catch their slaves back. Sometimes they would shoot at whoever
was trying to save the poor devils.

Mr. Rankins had a regular "station" for the slaves. He had a big lighthouse in his yard about thirty feet high, and he kept it burnin' all night.
It always meant freedom for a slave if he could get to this light.
Sometimes Mr. Rankins would have twenty or thirty slaves that had run
away on his place at a time. It must have cost him a whole lot to keep
'em and feed 'em, but I think some of his friends helped him.

Those who wanted to stay around that part of Ohio could stay, but
didn't many of them do it, because there was too much danger that you
would be walking along free one night, feel a hand over your mouth,
and be back across the river and in slavery again in the morning. And

nobody in the world ever got a chance to know as much misery as a slave that had escaped and been caught.

So a whole lot of them went on north to other parts of Ohio, or to New York, Chicago, or Canada. Canada was popular then because all of the slaves thought it was the last gate before you got all the way *inside* of Heaven. I don't think there was much chance for a slave to make a living in Canada, but didn't many of 'em come back. It seem like they rather starve up there in the cold than to be back in slavery.

The Army soon started taking a lot of 'em, too. They could enlist in the Union Army and get good wages, more food than they ever had, and have all the little gals wavin' at 'em when they passed. Them blue uniforms was a nice change, too.

I never got anything from a single one of the people I carried over the river to freedom. I didn't want anything. After I had made a few trips I got to like it, and even though I could have been free any night myself, I figgered I wasn't gettin' along so bad, so I would stay on Mr. Tabb's place and help the others get free. I did it for four years.

I don't know to this day how he never knew what I was doing. I used to take some awful chances, and he knew I must have been up to something. I wouldn't do much work in the day, would never be in my house at night, and when he would happen to visit the plantation where I had said I was goin', I wouldn't be there. Sometimes I think he did know and wanted me to get the slaves away that way so he wouldn't have to cause hard feelin's by freein' them.

I think Mr. Tabb used to talk a lot to Mr. John Fee. Mr. Fee was a man who lived in Kentucky, but Lord, how that man hated slavery! He used to always tell us—we never let our owners see us listenin' to him, though—that God didn't intend for some men to be free and some men to be in slavery. He used to talk to the owners, too, when they would listen to him, but mostly they hated the sight of John Fee.

In the night, though, he was a different man. For every slave who came through his place going across the river he had a good word, something to eat, and some kind of rags, too, if it was cold. He always knew just what to tell you to do if anything went wrong, and sometimes I think he kept slaves there on his place till they could be rowed across the river. Helped us a lot.

I almost ran the business in the ground after I had been carrying the slaves across for nearly four years. It was in 1863, and one night I carried across about twelve on the same night. Somebody must have seen us, because they set out after me as soon as I stepped out of the boat back on the Kentucky side. From that time on they were after me. Sometimes they would almost catch me. I had to run away from Mr. Tabb's plantation and live in the fields and in the woods. I didn't know what a bed was from one week to another. I would sleep in a cornfield tonight, up in the branches of a tree tomorrow night, and buried in a haypile the next night. The river, where I had carried so many across myself, was no good to me; it was watched too close.

Finally, I saw that I could never do any more good in Mason County, so I decided to take my freedom, too. I had a wife by this time, and one night we quietly slipped across and headed for Mr. Rankins' bell and light. It looked like we had to go almost to China to get across that river. I could hear the bell and see the light on Mr. Rankins' place, but the harder I rowed the farther away it got, and I knew if I didn't make it I'd get killed. But finally, I pulled up by the lighthouse, and went on to my freedom—just a few months before all of the slaves got theirs. I didn't stay in Ripley, though. I wasn't taking no chances. I went on to Detroit and still live there with most of my ten children and thirty-one grand-children.

The bigger ones don't care so much about hearin' it now, but the little ones never get tired of hearin' how their grandpa brought Emancipation to loads of slaves he could touch and feel, but never could see.

MARY ELLA GRANDBERRY

Interviewed at Sheffield, Alabama
Interviewed by Levi D. Shelby Jr.
Age when interviewed: 90

I DON'T know just how old I is, but I knows dat I'm somewheres nigh ninety years old. I was borned in Barton, Alabama. My father and mother come from Richmond, Virginny. My mammy was name Margaret Keller and my pappy was Adam Keller. My five sisters was Martha, Sarah, Harriet, Emma, and Rosanna, and my three brothers was Peter, Adam Jr., and William.

Us all live in a li'l two-room log cabin just off the Big House. Life weren't very much for us, 'cause we had to work and slave all de time. Massa Jim's house was a li'l old frame buildin' like a ordinary house is now. He was a single man and didn't have so terrible much, it seem. He had a whole lot, though, but just to look at him you'd think he was a poor white man. Dere was a lot o' cabins for de slaves, but dey wasn't fitten for nobody to live in. We just had to put up with 'em.

I don't 'member much about when I was a child. I disremembers ever playin' like chillens do today. Ever since I can 'member I had a water bucket on my arm totin' water to de hands. Iffen I weren't doin' dat, I was choppin' cotton. Chillens nowadays sees a good time to what we did den. Every mornin' just about hip of day de overseer was round to see dat we was ready to get to de fields. Plenty times us had to go withouten breakfast, 'cause we didn't get up in time to get it before de man done come to get us on de way to de field. Us worked till dinner time just de same before we got anything to eat.

De food we et was fixed just like it is now. My mammy fixed our grub at home. De only difference between den and now was us didn't get nothin' but common things den. Us didn't know what it was to get biscuits for breakfast every mornin'. It was corn bread till on Sundays, den us'd get four biscuits apiece. Us got fatback most every mornin'. Sometimes us might get chicken for dinner on a Sunday or some day like Christmas. It was mighty seldom us gets anything like dat, though.

We liked possums and rabbits but dey didn't come till winter time when some of de men folks'd run cross one in de field. Dey never had no chance to get out and hunt none.

Dere was no such thing as havin' different clothes for winter and summer. Us wore de same thing in summertime as in de winter time. De same was true about shoes. Us wore brogans from one year to de other.

My old marse was a pretty good man but nothin' extra. One thing about him, he wouldn't allow none of de overseers to whip none of us, lessen he was dere to see it done. Good thing he was like dat, too, 'cause he saved de blacks a many a lick what dey'd got iffen he hadn't been dere. Massa Jim was a bachelor, and he ain't never had much truck with womenfolks. Iffen he had any chillens, I never knowed nothin' about 'em.

De overseers was terrible hard on us. Dey'd ride up and down de field and haste you so till you near about fell out. Sometimes and most generally every time you behind de crowd you got a good lickin' with de bullwhip dat de driver had in de saddle with him. I heard Mammy say dat one day dey whipped poor Leah till she fall out like she was dead. Den dey rubbed salt and pepper on de blisters to make 'em burn real good. She was so sore till she couldn't lay on her back nights, and she just couldn't stand for no clothes to touch her back whatsoever.

Massa Jim had about one of de biggest plantations in dat section. I guess he had nigh onto a hundred blacks on de place. I never knowed 'zackly how many there was nor how big de place was.

De folks nowadays is always complainin' about how dey is havin' such hard times, but dey just don't know nothin'. Dey should have come up when I did and dey'd see now dey is livin' just like kings and queens. Dey don't have to get up before day when it's so dark you can just see your hands before your eyes. Dey don't know what it's like to have to keep up with de leader. You know dey was always somebody what could work faster dan de rest of de folks and dis fellow was always de leader, and everybody else was supposed to keep up with him or her whatsoever it was. Iffen you didn't keep up with de leader you got a good thrashin' when you gets home at night. It was always good dark when de hands got in from de field. 'Course, iffen dere was a lady what had a baby at home, she could leave just a little before de sun set.

Younguns nowadays don't know what it is to be punished; dey think iffen dey gets a li'l whippin' from dey mammy now dat dey is punish' terrible. Dey should of had to follow de leader for one day and see how dey'd be punish' iffen dey gets too far behind. De biggest thing dat us was punish' for was not keepin' up.

Dey'd whip us iffen we was caught talkin' about de free states, too. Iffen you weren't whipped, you was put in de "nigger box" and fed corn bread what was made withouten salt and with plain water. De box was just big 'nough for you to stand up in, but it had air holes in it to keep you from suffocatin'. Dere was plenty turnin' round room in it to allow you to change your position every once in a while. Iffen you had done a bigger 'nough thing you was kept in de "nigger box" for months at de time, and when you got out you was nothin' but skin and bones and scarcely able walk.

Half de time a slave didn't know dat he was sold till de massa'd call him to de Big House and tell him he had a new massa from den on. Every time dat one was sold de rest of 'em'd say, "I hopes next time'll be me." Dey thought you'd get a chance to run away to de free states. I heard my mammy say dat when she come from Virginny she come on a boat built outen logs. She say she never was so sick in all her life. I seed a whole wagon load of slaves come through our farm one day what was on dere way to Arkansas. Dey was most I ever seed travel at de same time.

De white folks didn't allow us to even look at a book. Dey would scold and sometimes whip us iffen dey caught us with our head in a book. Dat is one thing I surely did want to do and dat was to learn to read and write. Massa Jim promised to teach us to read and write, but he never had de time.

Dere weren't but one church on de place what I lived on, and de colored and de white both went to it. You know we was never allowed to go to church withouten some of de white folks with us. We weren't even allowed to talk with nobody from another farm. Iffen you did, you got one of de worst whippin's of your life. After freedom Massa Jim told us dat dey was 'fraid we'd get together and try to run away to de North, and dat dat was why dey didn't want us gettin' together talkin'.

A few years before de War my pappy learnt to read de Bible. Whenever we would go to church he would read to us and we'd sing. About de most two popular songs dey sung was "Steal Away" and "I Wonder Where Good Old Daniel Was." "Steal Away" is such a popular song what everybody knows it. De other one is done mighty nigh played out, so I'll sing it for you. It goes like dis:

> I wonder where was good old Daniel,
> I wonder where was good old Daniel,
> I wonder where was thinkin' Peter,
> I wonder where was thinkin' Peter.

> (Chorus)

> I'm goin' away, goin' away.
> I'm goin' away, goin' away,
> I wonder where was weepin' Mary,
> I wonder where was weepin' Mary,

I'm goin' away, I'm goin' away,
I'm goin' away to live forever,
I'll never turn back no more.

De slaves would get tired of de way dey was treated and try to run away to de North. I had a cousin to run away one time. Him and another fellow had got 'way up in Virginny before Massa Jim found out where dey was. Soon as Massa Jim found de whereabouts of George he went after him. When Massa Jim gets to George and 'em, George pretended like he didn't know Massa Jim. Massa Jim ask him, "George, don't you know me?" George he say, "I never seed you before in my life." Den dey ask George and 'em where did dey come from. George and dis other fellow look up in de sky and say, "I come from above, where all is love." Iffen dey had owned dey knowed Massa Jim he could have brung 'em back home. My pappy tried to get away de same time as George and dem did, but he couldn't see how to take all us chillen with him, so he had to stay with us. De blacks would slip off to de North and was caught and brung back. De paterrollers'd catch de colored folks and lock 'em up till de owner come after 'em.

Iffen a slave was cotched out after nine o'clock he was whipped. Dey didn't allow nobody out after it was dark, lessen he had a pass from de massa. One night, before George and dis fellow (I disremembers his name, but I think it was Ezra) runned away, George tried to get over to de bunk where he lived and one of de overseers seen him and dey put him in de "nigger box" for three weeks. Just as soon as he got out again, George and dis Ezra slipped off. Dey had a sign dat dey would give each other every night after sundown. George would hang de lantern in de window, and den he would take it outen de window and hang it right back in dere again. I couldn't never make no sense outen it. I asked him one day what he was a-doin' dat for. He say dat before long I'd know 'zackly what it all about. Dis was de sign of how long dey have to wait before dey try to get away.

After de day's work was over, de slaves didn't have nothin' to do but to go to bed. In fact, dey didn't feel like doin' nothin' else. On Saturday dey set up and washed so's dey could have some clean clothes to wear de comin' week. We worked all day, every day 'ceptin' some Saturdays, we had a half day off den. Us didn't get many and only when us asked for 'em. On Sundays us just laid round most all day. Us didn't get no pleasure outen goin' to church, 'cause we weren't allowed to say nothin'. Sometimes, even on Christmas, us didn't get no rest. I 'members on one Christmas us had to build a lime kiln. When us get a holiday us rested. Iffen dere was a weddin' or a funeral on our plantation us went. Otherways we don't go nowhere.

De War come when I was a big gal. I 'member dat my uncle and cousin joined in with de Yankees to help fight for de freedom. De Yankees come to our place and runned Massa Jim away and took de house for a hospital. Dey took all of Massa Jim's clothes and gived dem to some of dere friends. Dey burned up all de cotton, hay, peas, and everything dat was in de barns. Dey made de white folks cook for de colored and den serve 'em while dey et. De Yankees made 'em do for us like we done for dem. Dey showed de white folks what it was to work for somebody else. Dey stayed on our place for de longest. When dey did leave, dere weren't a mouthful to eat in de house. When de War was over, Massa Jim told us dat we had to find somewheres else to live. 'Course, some of my folks had already gone when he come home. Us left Massa Jim's and moved to another farm. We got pay for de work what we did on dis other place.

Right after de War de Ku Klux got after de colored folks. Dey would come to our houses and scare us most to death. Dey would take some of de niggers out and whip 'em and dose dat dey didn't whip dey tied up by dere fingers and toes. Dese Ku Klux would come to our windows at night and say: "Your time ain't long a-comin'." De Ku Klux got so bad dat dey would even get us in de daytime. Dey kept dis up till some folks from de North come down and put a stop to it.

I married Nelson Grandberry. De weddin' was private. I don't have no chillens, but my husband got four. I haven't heered from any of 'em in a long time now. I guess dey all dead.

SARAH GUDGER

Interviewed in Asheville, North Carolina
Interviewed by Marjorie Jones
Age when interviewed: 121

I WAS born about two miles from Old Fort on de Old Morgantown Road. I sure has had a hard life. Just work and work and work. I never know nothin' but work. My boss he was Ole Man Andy Hemphill. He had a large plantation in de valley. Plenty of everythin'. All kind of stock: hogs, cows, mules, and hosses. When Marse Andy die I got live with he son, William Hemphill. I never forget when Marse Andy die. He was a good ole man, and de Missie she was good, too. She used to read de Bible to us chillen afore she pass away.

My pappy, he live with Joe Gudger. He old and feeble, I 'members. He depend on my pappy to see after everythin' for him. He always trust my pappy. One mornin' he follow Pappy to de field. Pappy he stop his work and Ole Marse Joe, he say: "Well, Smart (Pappy, he name Smart), I'se tired, worried, and troubled. All dese years I work for my chillen. Dey never do de right thing. Dey worries me, Smart. I tell you, Smart, I'se a good mind to put myself away. I'se a good mind to drown myself right here. I terrible worried, Smart."

Pappy, he take hold Old Marse Joe and lead him to de house. "Now Marse Joe, I wouldn't talk such talk iffen I'se you. You been good to you family. Just you content yo'self and rest." But a few days after dat, Ole Marse Joe was found a-hangin' in de barn by de bridle. Ole Marse had put heself away.

I never knowed what it was to rest. I just work all de time from mornin' till late at night. I had to do everythin' dey was to do on de outside. Work in de field, chop wood, hoe corn, till sometime I feels like my back surely break. I done everythin' 'cept split rails. You know, dey split rails back in dem days. Well, I never did split no rails.

Ole Marse strop us good if we did anythin' he didn't like. Sometime he get his dander up and den we dassent look round at him, else he tie you hands afore you body and whip you, just like you a mule. Lordy,

66

I'se took a thousand lashin's in my day. Sometimes my poor old body be sore for a week.

Ole Boss he send us niggers out in any kind of weather, rain or snow, it never matter. We had to go to de mountains, cut wood and drag it down to de house. Many de time we come in with our clothes stuck to our poor old cold bodies, but 'twarn't no use to try to get 'em dry. If de Old Boss or de Ole Missie see us dey yell: "Get on out of here, you black thing, and get you work out of de way!" And we knowed to get, else we get de lash. Dey didn't care how old or how young you were, you never too big to get de lash.

De rich white folks never did no work; dey had darkies to do it for dem. In de summer we had to work outdoors, in de winter in de house. I had to card and spin till ten o'clock. Never get much rest, had to get up at four de next mornin' and start again. Didn't get much to eat, neither, just a li'l corn bread and 'lasses. Lordy, you cain't know what a time I had. All cold and hungry. I ain't tellin' no lies. It de gospel truth. It sure is.

I 'member well how I used to lie awake till all de folks was sleepin', den creep out of de door and walk barefoot in de snow, about two miles to my ole auntie's house. I knowed when I get dere she fix hot corn pone with slice o' meat and some milk for me to eat. Auntie was good to us darkies.

I never sleep on a bedstead till after freedom. Just an old pile o' rags in de corner. Hardly 'nough to keep us from freezin'. Law, nobody knows how mean darkies was treated. Why, dey was better to de animals dan to us. My first Ole Marse was a good ole man, but de last one, he was rapid—he sure was rapid.

Weren't none o' de slaves offen our plantation ever sold, but de ones on de other plantation of Marse William were. Oh, dat was a terrible time! All de slaves be in de field, plowin', hoein', and singin' in de boilin' sun. Ole Marse, he come through de field with a man call de speculator. Dey walked round just lookin', just lookin'. All de darkies know what dis mean. Dey didn't dare look up, just work right on. Den de speculator he see who he want. He talk to Ole Marse, den dey slaps de handcuffs on him and take him away to de cotton country.

Oh, dem was awful times! When de speculator was ready to go with de slaves, if dere was anyone who didn't want to go, he thrash 'em, den tie 'em behind de wagon and make 'em run till dey fall on de ground, den he thrash 'em till dey say dey go without no trouble. Sometime some of dem run away and come back to de plantation, den it was harder on dem dan before. When de darkies went to dinner de ole nigger mammy she ask where am such and such. None of de others want to tell her. But when she see dem look down to de ground she just say:

"De speculator, de speculator." Den de tears roll down her cheeks, cause maybe it her son or husband and she know she never see 'em again. Maybe dey leaves babies to home, maybe just pappy and mammy. Oh, my lordy, my ole boss was mean, but he never sent us to de cotton country.

Dey was very few schools back in dat day and time, very few. We darkies didn't dare look at no book, not even to pick it up. Ole Missie, dat is, my first ole missie, she was a good ole woman. She read to de niggers and to de white chillun. She come from 'cross de water. She weren't like de smart white folks livin' here now. When she come over here she brung darky boy with her. He was her personal servant. 'Course, dey got different names for dem now, but in dat day dey calls 'em "Guinea niggers." She was good ole woman, not like other white folks. Niggers like Ole Missie.

When de darkies get sick, dey were put in a li'l ole house close to de Big House, and one of de other darkies waited on 'em. Dere were very few doctors den. Only three in de whole section. When dey wanted medicine dey went to de woods and gathered horehound, slippery elm for poultices, and all kinds bark for teas. All dese herbs bring you round.

I 'members when my ole mammy die. She lived on Reems Creek with other Hemphills. She sick long time. One day white man come to see me. He say: "Sarah, did you know you mammy was dead?" "No," I say, "but I wants to see my mother afore dey puts her away." I went to de house and say to Ole Missie: "My mother she die today. I wants to see my mother afore dey puts her away," but she look at me mean and say: "Get on out of here, and get back to you work afore I wallop you good." So I went back to my work, with the tears streamin' down my face, just a-wringin' my hands, I wanted to see my mammy so. About two weeks later, Ole Missie she get terrible sick. She just linger along for long time, but she never gets up no more. Weren't long afore dey puts her away, too, just like my mammy.

I 'members de time when my mammy was alive, I was a small child, afore dey took her to Reems Creek. All us chillens was playin' in de yard one night. Just a-runnin' and a-playin' like chillen will. All of a sudden Mammy come to de door all 'cited. "Come in here dis minute," she say. "Just look up at what is a-happenin'." And, bless you life, de stars were fallin' just like rain. Mammy was terrible scared, but we chillen weren't afraid, no we weren't afraid. But Mammy, she say every time a star fall, somebody gonna die. Look like a lot of folks gonna die from de looks of dem stars. Everythin' was just as bright as day. You could of pick a pin up. You know de stars don't shine as bright as dey did back den. Weren't long afore dey took my mammy away, and I was left alone.

On de plantation was an ole woman what de boss bought from a drover up in Virginny. De boss he bought her from one of de speculators. She laugh and tell us: "Some of dese days yo'all gwine be free, just like de white folks," but we all laugh at her. No, we just slaves, we always have to work and never be free. Den when freedom come, she say: "I told yo'all, now you got no learnin', you got nothin', got no home; what you gwine do? Didn't I tell you?"

I was gettin' along smartly in years when de War come. I 'member just like yesterday just afore de War. Marse William was a-talkin' to his brother. I was standin' off a piece. Marse's brother, he say: "William, how old Aunt Sarah now?" Marse William look at me and he say: "She's gettin' nigh on to fifty." Dat was just a li'l while afore de War.

Dat was awful time. Us darkies didn't know what it was all about. Only one of de boys from de plantation go. He Alexander, he about twenty-five den. Many de time we get word de Yankees comin'. We take our food and stock and hide it till we sure dey's gone. We weren't bothered much. One day, I never forget, we look out and see soldiers marchin'; look like de whole valley full of dem. I thought: "Poor helpless critters, just goin' away to get kilt." De drums were beatin' and de fifes a-playin'. Dey were de foot company. Oh, glory, it was a sight! Sometime dey come home on furlough. Sometime dey get kilt afore dey gets through. Alexander, he come home a few times afore freedom.

When de War was over, Marse William he say: "Did yo'all know yo'all's free. You free now." I chuckle, 'membering what de ole woman tell us about freedom, and no learnin'. Lots o' men want me to go to foreign land, but I tell 'em I go live with my pappy, long as he live. I stay with de white folks about twelve months, den I stay with my pappy long as he live.

MARTIN JACKSON

Interviewed at San Antonio, Texas
Interviewer not identified
Age when interviewed: 90

I HAVE about eighty-five years of good memory to call on. I'm ninety, and so I'm not counting my first five years of life. I'll try to give you as clear a picture as I can. If you want to give me a copy of what you are going to write, I'll appreciate it. Maybe some of my children would like to have it.

I was here in Texas when the Civil War was first talked about. I was here when the War started and followed my young master into it with the First Texas Cavalry. I was here during Reconstruction, after the War. I was here during the European World War and the second week after the United States declared war on Germany I enlisted as cook at Camp Leon Springs.

This sounds as if I liked the war racket. But, as a matter of fact, I never wore a uniform—gray coat or khaki coat—or carried a gun, unless it happened to be one worth saving after some Confederate soldier got shot. I was official lugger-in of men that got wounded, and might have been called a Red Cross worker if we had had such a corps connected with our company. My father was head cook for the battalion and between times I helped him out with the mess. There was some difference in the food served to soldiers in 1861 and 1917!

Just what my feelings was about the War, I have never been able to figure out myself. I knew the Yanks were going to win, from the beginning. I wanted them to win and lick us Southerners, but I hoped they was going to do it without wiping out our company. I'll come back to that in a minute. As I said, our company was the First Texas Cavalry. Colonel Buchell was our commander. He was a full-blooded German and as fine a man and a soldier as you ever saw. He was killed at the Battle of Marshall and died in my arms. You may also be interested to know that my old master, Alvy Fitzpatrick, was the grandfather of Governor Jim Ferguson.

Lots of old slaves closes the door before they tell the truth about their days of slavery. When the door is open, they tell how kind their masters was and how rosy it all was. You can't blame them for this, because they had plenty of early discipline, making them cautious about saying anything uncomplimentary about their masters. I, myself, was in a little different position than most slaves and, as a consequence, have no grudges or resentment. However, I can tell you the life of the average slave was not rosy. They were dealt out plenty of cruel suffering.

Even with my good treatment, I spent most of my time planning and thinking of running away. I could have done it easy, but my old father used to say, "No use running from bad to worse, hunting better." Lots of colored boys did escape and joined the Union army, and there are plenty of them drawing pension today. My father was always counseling me. He said, "Every man has to serve God under his own vine and fig tree." He kept pointing out that the War wasn't going to last forever, but that our forever was going to be spent living among the Southerners, after they got licked. He'd cite examples of how the whites would stand flat-footed and fight for the blacks the same as for members of their own family. I knew that all was true, but still I rebelled, from inside of me. I think I really was afraid to run away, because I thought my conscience would haunt me. My father knew I felt this way and he'd rub my fears in deeper. One of his remarks still rings in my ears: "A clear conscience opens bowels, and when you have a guilty soul it ties you up and death will not for long desert you."

I haven't had any education. I should have had one, though. My old missus was sorry, after the War, that she didn't teach me. Her name, before she married my old master, was Mrs. Long. She lived in New York City and had three sons. When my old master's wife died, he wrote up to a friend of his in New York, a very prominent merchant named C. C. Stewart. He told this friend he wanted a wife and gave him specifications for one. Well, Mrs. Long, whose husband had died, fitted the bill and she was sent down to Texas. She became Mrs. Fitzpatrick. She wasn't the grandmother of Governor Ferguson. Old Fitzpatrick had two wives that preceded Mrs. Long. One of the wives had a daughter named Fanny Fitzpatrick and it was her that was the Texas governor's mother. I seem to have the complicated family tree of my old master more clear than I've got my own, although mine can be put in a nutshell! I married only once and was blessed in it with forty-five years of devotion. I had thirteen children and a big crop of grandchildren.

My earliest recollection is the day my old boss presented me to his son, Joe, as his property. I was about five years old and my new master was only two.

It was in the Battle of Marshall, in Louisiana, that Colonel Buchell got shot. I was about three miles from the front, where I had pitched up a kind of first-aid station. I was all alone there. I watched the whole thing. I could hear the shooting and see the firing. I remember standing there and thinking the South didn't have a chance. All of a sudden I heard someone call. It was a soldier, who was half carrying Colonel Buchell in. I didn't do nothing for the Colonel. He was too far gone. I just held him comfortable, and that was the position he was in when he stopped breathing. That was the worst hurt I got when anybody died. He was a friend of mine. He had had a lot of soldiering before and fought in the Indian War.

Well, the Battle of Marshall broke the back of the Texas Cavalry. We began straggling back towards New Orleans, and by that time the War was over. The soldiers began to scatter. They was a sorry-lookin' bunch of lost sheep. They didn't know where to go, but most of 'em ended up pretty close to the towns they started from. They was like homing pigeons, with only the instinct to go home and, yet, most of them had no homes to go to.

I never went into books. I used to handle a big dictionary three times a day, but it was only to put it on a chair so my young master could sit up higher at the table. I never went to school. I learned to talk pretty good by associating with my masters in their Big House.

We lived on a ranch of about one thousand acres close to the Jackson County line in Victoria County, about 125 miles from San Antonio. Just before the War ended they sold the ranch, slaves and all, and the family, not away fighting, moved to Galveston. Of course, my father and me wasn't sold with the other blacks because we was away at war.

My mother was drowned years before when I was a little boy. I only remember her after she was dead. I can take you to the spot in the river today where she was drowned. She drowned herself. I never knew the reason behind it, but it was said she started to lose her mind and preferred death to that.

The master's name was usually adopted by a slave after he was set free. This was done more because it was the logical thing to do and the easiest way to be identified than it was through affection for the master. Also, the government seemed to be in a almighty hurry to have us get names. We had to register as someone, so we could be citizens. Well, I got to thinking about all us slaves that was going to take the name Fitzpatrick. I made up my mind I'd find me a different one. One of my grandfathers in Africa was called Jeaceo, and so I decided to be Jackson.

SILAS JACKSON

Interviewed at Baltimore, Maryland
Interviewed by _____ Rogers
Age when interviewed: 90

I was born at or near Ashbie's Gap in Virginia, either in the year 1846 or '47. I do not know which, but I will say I am ninety years of age. My father's name was Sling and mother's Sarah Louis. They were purchased by my master from a slave trader in Richmond, Virginia. My father was a man of large stature and my mother was tall and stately. They originally came from the eastern shore of Maryland, I think from the Legg estate; beyond that I do not know. I had three brothers and two sisters. My brothers were older than I, and my sisters younger. Their names were Silas, Carter, Rap or Raymond, I do not remember; my sisters were Jane and Susie, both of whom are living in Virginia now. Only one I have ever seen and he came North with General Sherman. He died in 1925. He was a Baptist minister like myself.

The only thing I know about my grandparents were: My grandfather ran away through the aid of Harriet Tubman and went to Philadelphia and saved three hundred and fifty dollars, and purchased my grandmother through the aid of a Quaker or an Episcopal minister, I do not know. I have on several occasions tried to trace this part of my family's past history, but without success.

I was a large boy for my age. When I was nine years of age my tasks began and continued until 1864. In Virginia where I was, they raised tobacco, wheat, corn, and farm products. I have had a taste of all the work on the farm, besides digging and clearing up new ground to increase the acreage to the farm. We all had task work to do—men, women, and boys. We began work on Monday and worked until Saturday. That day we were allowed to work for ourselves and to garden or to do extra work. When we could get work, or work on someone else's place, we got a pass from the overseer to go off the plantation, but to be back by nine o'clock on Saturday night or when cabin inspection was made. Sometimes we could earn as much as fifty cents a day, which we used to buy cakes, candies, or clothes.

On Saturday each slave was given ten pounds of cornmeal, a quart of blackstrap [molasses], six pounds of fatback, three pounds of flour and vegetables, all of which were raised on the farm. All of the slaves hunted, or those who wanted to, hunted rabbits, opossums, or fished. These were our choice food as we did not get anything special from the overseer. Our food was cooked by our mothers or sisters and, for those who were not married, by the old women and men assigned for that work. Each family was given three acres to raise their chickens or vegetables, and if a man raised his own food he was given ten dollars at Christmas time extra, besides his presents.

In the summer or when warm weather came each slave was given something; the women, linsey goods or gingham clothes; the men overalls, muslin shirts, top and underclothes, two pair of shoes, and a straw hat to work in. In the cold weather, we wore woolen clothes, all made at the sewing cabin.

My master was named Tom Ashbie, a meaner man was never born in Virginia—brutal, wicked, and hard. He always carried a cowhide with him. If he saw anyone doing something that did not suit his taste, he would have the slave tied to a tree, man or woman, and then would cowhide the victim until he got tired, or sometimes, the slave would faint.

Mrs. Ashbie was kind and lovely to her slaves when Mr. Ashbie was out. The Ashbies did not have any children of their own, but they had boys and girls of his own sister and they were much like him. They had maids or private waiters for the young men if they wanted them.

I have heard it said by people in authority, Tom Ashbie owned nine thousand acres of farmland besides woodland. He was a large slave owner, having more than a hundred slaves on his farm. They were awakened by blowing of the horn before sunrise by the overseer, started work at sunrise and worked all day to sundown, with no time to go to the cabin for dinner. You carried your dinner with you. The slaves were driven at top speed and whipped at the snap of the finger by the overseers. We had four overseers on the farm, all hired white men. I have seen men beaten until they dropped in their tracks; or knocked over by clubs; women stripped down to their waist and cowhided.

I have heard it said that Tom Ashbie's father went to one of the cabins late at night. The slaves was having a secret prayer meeting. He heard one slave ask God to change the heart of his master and deliver him from slavery so that he may enjoy freedom. Before the next day the man disappeared, no one ever seeing him again. But after that down in the swamp, at certain times of the moon, you could hear the man who prayed in the cabin praying. When old man Ashbie died, just before he died, he told the white Baptist minister that he had killed Zeke for praying and that he was going to hell.

The Ashbies' home was a large stone mansion, with a porch on three sides, wide halls in the center up and downstairs, numerous rooms and a stone kitchen built on the back connected with the dining room. There was a stone building on the farm. It is there today. I saw it this summer while visiting in Virginia. The old jail, it is now used as a garage. Downstairs there were two rooms, one where some of the whipping was done, and the other used by the overseer. Upstairs was used for women and girls. The iron bars have corroded, but you can see where they were. I have never seen slaves sold on the farm, but I have seen them taken away and brought there. Several times I have seen slaves chained taken away and chained when they came.

No one on the place was taught to read or write. On Sunday the slaves who wanted to worship would gather at one of the large cabins with one of the overseers present and have their church, after which the overseer would talk. When communion was given the overseer was paid for staying there with half of the collection taken up, sometimes he would get twenty-five cents. No one could read the Bible. Sandy Jasper, Mr. Ashbie's coachman, was the preacher. He would go to the white Baptist church on Sunday with the family and would be better informed because he heard the white preacher.

Twice each year, after harvest and after New Year's, the slaves would have their protracted meeting, or their revival, and after each closing they would baptize in the creek. Sometimes in the winter they would break the ice singing "Going to the Water" or some other hymn of that nature. And at each funeral, the Ashbies would attend the service conducted in the cabin where the deceased was, from there taking him to the slave graveyard. A lot dedicated for that purpose was situated about three-fourths of a mile from the cabins, near a hill.

There were a number of slaves on our plantation who ran away. Some were captured and sold to a Georgia trader, others were never captured. To intimidate the slaves, the overseers were connected with the patrollers, not only to watch our slaves, but sometimes for the rewards for other slaves who had run away from other plantations. This feature caused a great deal of trouble between the whites and blacks. In 1858, two white men were murdered near Warrenton on the road, by colored people. It was never known whether by free people or slaves.

When work was done the slaves retired to their cabins. Some played games, others cooked or rested or did what they wanted. We did not work on Saturdays unless in harvest times, then Saturdays were days of work. At other times, on Saturdays you were at leisure to do what you wanted. On Christmas day, Mr. Ashbie would call all the slaves together, give them presents, money, after which they spent the day as they liked. On New Year's day, we all were scared—that was the time for selling, buying, and trading slaves. We did not know who was to go or come.

LEWIS JENKINS

Interviewed in Oklahoma City, Oklahoma
Interviewed by Ida Belle Hunter
Age when interviewed: 93

I WAS born in Green County, Alabama in January 1844. My mother was a white woman, and her name was Jane Jenkins. My father was a nigger. He was a coachman on my master's place. I was told this in 1880 by the white doctor, Lyth Smith, which brung me into the world. My master, who was my grandfather, brung me to Texas when I was just seven or eight years old. A few years later, he brung my mother down to Texas, and she had with her three boys, which was her chillen and my brothers. They was white chillen and named Jones. They first names was Tom, Joe, and Lije. They parted from me and I never heerd no more about 'em. I didn't even know my mother when I seen her. All my life I done just knowed my white kinfolks and nothing at all about the other part of my color.

Before I was born, my mother was taken away from her playmates and kept in the attic hid. They took me soon as I was born from her. When her time to be in bed was up, she'd ask the waitman where I was at. The waitman was Dr. Lyth Smith. He'd tell her I was at Ann's house. I never got a chance to nurse my mother. After she got up and come down, she wanted to see her baby. Now she goes to Ann's house and couldn't find me. After she couldn't find me there, she looked in all the houses on the place for me, her baby. Then she commenced screaming, tearing her clothes off and tearing her hair out. They sent her to the calaboose till they could get some clothes to put on. She went distracted. She tore out towards town. The way they got her to hush, they told her I was with my grandma. They had me hid on the road to Texas. The doctor's wife said I was the first nigger she shed a tear over. It was a destruction thing.

Well, that scandalized the family, and they moved to Texas and come by and got me and took me to Texas. When they crossed the Tom Bigby River in Alabama, three miles wide, on boat, this woman that had me

77

in hand, was just churning me up and down in the river. They hollered at her, and I says that's where God took me in his bosom. When I was seven or eight years old, the white folks took me in charge. They was gonna make me a watchman to watch for 'em at night. But when they begun this, I wasn't old enough to remember.

The first house I was sent to was the cook's house. The cook said, "What you come down here for?" I told her I didn't know. "Who sent you?" I said, "Old Master Jenkins." She knowed 'mediately what I was sent for, don't you see? She says to me, "Sit down, little rascal," with her fist drawn back, "I'll knock you in the head." Well, what could I do but sit, childlike? Before long I was asleep, and they took me outdoors. Next morning I was told to go to the big house. Old Master asked me, "What'd you see last night?" I told him I didn't seed nothing. Now they got the cowhide and hit me three or four licks and asked that same question again. I told 'em I didn't seed nothing. This went on for 'bout a hour. I had to take a whipping every morning 'cause I had to go to every house and never seen nothing. The last house I went to, well, in the morning as I was going back to the big house, a voice came to me and said, "See nothing, tell nothing." It meant for me not to lie, and on and on as I growed for years to come, I was big enough to plow corn, I was out in the field, ad a voice—that same voice, too—said, "Iffen I was you, I'd leave this place 'cause you'll come to want and won't have." All this was the causing of my conversion.

My first job was scouring floors, and I mean I scoured 'em, too. Next, I scoured knives and forks. From that job I went to real work and no play.

My master and his family just lived in a log house. My mistress was my grandfather's wife and my grandmother, but I couldn't claim her. Her and her oldest child treated me some rough. I never had no good time till that old white woman died, and talking 'bout somebody glad she died, I sure was. They took turns treating me badly.

There was 'bout twenty slaves on our place, chillen and all. Dewan, which was my uncle, was the overseer. He waked us up just before sunrise, and we worked from sun to sun. I seen 'em tie niggers hand and foot to mill posts and whip 'em with bullwhips. Them was neighbors, though, not our'n. They whipped the women by pulling they dresses down to they hips and beat 'em till they was satisfied. For myself, my grandfather whipped me till his dog took pity on me and tried to drag me away. This is the scar on my leg where he pulled on me. He was beating me till I said, "Oh, pray, Master!"

I seen 'em sell people what wasn't able to work from the block just like cattle. They would be chained together. They took mothers from chillen even just a week old and sell 'em. They stripped the slaves, women and all, and let the bidders look at 'em to see iffen they was scarred before they would buy 'em.

Them old white folks wouldn't learn us to read and write and wouldn't let they young'uns learn us. My youngest mistress, which was my auntie, mind you, was trying to learn me to read and write and was caught, and she got some whipping, almost a killing.

I never seen but one nigger man hung. He was crippled and had run away. I seen this with my own eyes, no guesswork. He had caught a little white girl, schoolgirl, too, ravaged her, and cut her tongue off. Oh, that was barbarous. He oughta been burnt. He didn't get his just due at hanging.

Patrollers was sure through the country. They was out to keep down nigger and white mixing and to keep niggers from having liberty to go out, 'specially at night. They didn't allow you to come to see a gal 'less she was eighteen and you was twenty-one. The cause of this was to raise good stock. The gals couldn't marry till they was eighteen, neither, but they could have chillen. You had to have a pass to see your gal, even. Now you got your pass from your master. Iffen you was under fifteen, you could go play and didn't need no pass, but all over fifteen just had to have a pass.

They would go right to bed after they ate. No Saturday off, just washday off. Some Sundays Old Mistress let us have sugar, flour, and lard, but just some Sundays; no other day, though.

We was in great game country and sure ate our fill of coons, possums, rabbits, deer, turkeys, and the such and things people wouldn't notice now. Corn bread and sweet potatoes was my favorite foods. Milk and butter was best eating.

We just wore what you call slips with just two sleeves slipped over our head. No buttons. We wore the same thing in winter, just heavier. Never wore no shoes till I was old enough to chop cotton. At weddings they wore stripes all the time. They made 'em on hand looms. They was mostly white and red stripes.

We played marbles and ring plays. We used to sing this ditty during playing:

> So many pretty gals,
> So they say.
> So many pretty gals,
> So they say.
> Just peep through the window, Susie gal.

We used onions to keep off consumption. There was a family taken by the black disease and they all died but one, and he was ready to die.

They took him out to burn the house up to keep that disease from spreading. They put the nigger in a house full of onions, and he sure 'nough got well. The doctor said the onions had cured him. We believed in our onions and do till today. Even the next morning after he was put in the house and could work, he asked for some milk.

That war that freed the niggers started in 1861. I had two young masters to go. It lasted four years. They was figuring on taking me that very next year, and it was so fixed that the war ended. We had a big drought during the war, which made it bad on the soldiers. I never seen the Yankees only when they was passing along the road. One day whilst we was eating our dinner, our master said, "All yo'all, young and old, when you get through, come out on the gallery (we call 'em porches now). I got something to tell you." When we got through, we all trooped out, and he said, "This is military law, but I am forced to tell you." He says, "This law says free the nigger, so now you is just as free as me by this law. I can't make yo' all stay with me unless you want to. Therefore you can go anyplace you want to." That was 'bout laying-by drop time in June. It was on June 19th, and we still celebrates that day in Texas— that is "Nigger Day" down there. He said, "I'd like for you to stay till the crops is laid by, iffen you will." Iffen it hadn't been for his wife maybe we would have stayed on, but she just kept bossing the nigger women, and we just didn't like it, and that's what brung on the scatter. I left my old master and went with one of my young masters, which was my uncle.

I was sure once tickled at my young master. I done broke in a mule for him, and he got on him one night to join the Ku Klux band. He had to go 'bout four miles. He got just 'bout one mile, and they come to two trees with a real white stone in 'twixt the trees. The mule seen this and throwed my master off and hurt him something terrible. He come back and told his wife what done happened. He said, "Damn the Ku Klux." He never went to join 'em no more.

I never went to school in my life. Never had the opportunity 'cause I never had no kinfolks who own me give me advice or help me. White kinfolks just bossed me. I was just like an orphan. White folks will mess you up and be so treacherous.

I married Jane Deckers. The white man just read out of the Bible and put our names and ages in the Bible, and that was all the ceremony we had. I got three chillen and four grandchillen. One do stone work, another brick work, and my daughter, housework.

I think Abe Lincoln was next to Jesus Christ. The best human man ever lived. He died helping the poor nigger man. Old Jeff Davis right in his place. He was trying to help his race. He wasn't nothing like right. It was God's plan that every man be free. I don't believe Davis believed in right. I am sure glad slavery is over. I glory in it. I trust and pray it'll never be again.

I think the church is the gospel way and everybody ought to be in it. The Baptist is my dear belief, 'cause I was baptized by the spirit and then by the water, nothing but the Baptist. I belongs to the Shiloh Baptist Church, right here on the west side.

TINES KENDRICKS

Interviewed at Trenton, Arkansas
Interviewed by Watt McKinney
Age when interviewed: 104

MY NAME is Tines Kendricks. I was borned in Crawford County, Georgia. You see, Boss, I is a little nigger, and I really is more smaller now dan I used to be when I was young 'cause I so old and stooped over. I mighty nigh wore out from all dese hard years of work and serving de Lord. My actual name what was given to me by my white folks, de Kendricks, was "Tiny." Dey called me dat 'cause I never was no size much. After us all set free I just changed my name to "Tines" and dat's what I been goin' by for nigh on to ninety years.

'Cordin' to what I remember about it, Boss, I is now past a hundred and four year old this past July de fourth two hours before day. What I means is what I remember about what de old master told me dat time I comed back to de home place after de War quit and he say dat I past thirty den. My mammy, she said I born two hours before day on de fourth of July. Dat what dey told me, Boss. I has been in good health all my days. I ain't never been sick any in my life 'scusing dese last years, when I get so old and feeble and stiff in de joints, and my teeth began to cave, and my old bones, dey begin to ache. But I just keep on living and trusting in de Lord 'cause de Good Book say, "Wherefore de evil days come and de darkness of de night draw nigh, your strength, it shall not perish. I will lift you up amongst dem what abides with me." Dat is de Gospel, Boss.

My old master, he was named Arch Kendricks, and us lived on de plantation what de Kendricks had not far from Macon in Crawford County, Georgia. You can see, Boss, dat I is a little bright and got some white blood in me. Dat is accounted for on my mammy's side of de family. Her pappy, he was a white man. He wasn't no Kendrick though. He was an overseer. Dat what my mammy she say, and den I know dat wasn't no Kendrick mixed up in nothing like dat. Dey didn't believe in dat kind of business. My old master, Arch Kendricks, I will say this, he

82

certainly was a good fair man. Old Miss and de young master, Sam, dey was strictly tough, and, Boss, I is telling you de truth, dey was cruel. De young master, Sam, he never taken at all after he pa. He got all he meanness from Old Miss, and he sure got plenty of it too. Old Miss, she cuss and rare worse dan a man. Way 'fore day she be up hollerin' loud enough for to be heard two miles, 'rousing de niggers out for to get in de fields even 'fore light. Master Sam, he stand by de pots handing out de grub and giving out de bread, and he cuss loud and say: "Take a sop of dat grease on your hoecake and move along fast 'fore I lashes you." Master Sam, he was a big man too, dat he was. He was nigh on to six and a half feet tall. Boss, he certainly was a child of de devil.

All de cooking in dem days was done in pots hanging on de pot racks. Dey never had no stoves during de times what I is telling you about. At times dey would give us enough to eat. At times dey wouldn't—just according to how dey feeling when dey dishing out de grub. De biggest what dey would give de field hands to eat would be de truck what us had on de place, like greens, turnips, peas, side meat, and dey sure would cut de side meat awful thin too, Boss. Us always had a heap of cornmeal dumplings and hoecakes. Old Miss, her and Master Sam, dey real stingy. You better not leave no grub on your plate for to throw away. You sure better eat it all if you like it or no. Old Miss and Master Sam, dey de real bosses, and dey was wicked. I'se tellin' you de truth, dey was. Old Master, he didn't have much to say about de running of de place or de handling of de niggers. You know all de property and all de niggers belonged to Old Miss. She got all dat from her peoples. Dat what dey left to her on dere death. She de real owner of everything.

Just to show you, Boss, how 'twas with Master Sam, and how contrary and fractious and wicked dat young white man was, I wants to tell you about de time dat Aunt Hannah's little boy Mose died. Mose, he sick about a week. Aunt Hannah, she try to doctor on him and get him well, and she tell Old Miss dat she think Mose bad off and ought to have de doctor. Old Miss, she wouldn't get de doctor. She say Mose ain't sick much, and bless my soul, Aunt Hannah she right. In a few days from den, Mose is dead. Master Sam, he come cussing and told Gabe to get some planks and make de coffin and sent some of dem to dig de grave over dere on de far side of de place where dey had a burying-ground for de niggers. Us toted de coffin over to where de grave was dug and going to bury little Mose dere, and Uncle Billy Jordan he was dere and begun to sing and pray and have a kind of funeral at de burying. Everyone was moaning and singing and praying and Master Sam heard dem and come sailing over dere on he hoss and lit right in to cussing and raring and say dat if dey don't hurry and bury dat nigger and shut up dat singing and carrying on, he going to lash every one of dem, and den he

went to cussing worser and abusing Uncle Billy Jordan. He say if he
ever hear of him doing any more preaching or praying around 'mongst
de niggers at de graveyard or anywhere else, he going to lash him to
death. No sir, Boss, Master Sam wouldn't even allow no preaching or
singing or nothing like dat. He was wicked. I tell you he was.

Old Miss, she generally looked after de niggers when dey sick and
gave dem de medicine. And too, she would get de doctor if she think
dey real bad off 'cause, like I said, Old Miss, she mighty stingy and she
never want to lose no nigger by dem dying. However, it was hard sometime to get her to believe you sick when you tell her dat you was, and
she would think you just playing off from work. I have seen niggers
what would be mighty near dead before Old Miss would believe dem
sick at all.

Before de War broke out, I can remember dere was some few of de
white folks what said dat niggers ought to be set free, but dere was just
one now and den dat took dat stand. One of dem dat I remember was
de Reverend Dickey what was de parson for a big crowd of de white
peoples in dat part of de county. Reverend Dickey, he preached freedom for de niggers and say dat dey all should be set free and gived a
home and a mule. Dat preaching de Reverend Dickey done sure did
rile up de folks—dat is, most of dem like de Kendricks and Mr.
Eldredge and Dr. Murcheson and Nat Walker and such as dem what
was de biggest of de slaveowners. Right away after Reverend Dickey
done such preaching, dey fired him from de church, and abused him,
and some of dem say dey going to hang him to a limb, or either going
to ride him on a rail out of de country. Sure enough, dey made it so hot
on dat man he have to leave clean out of de state so I heared. No sir,
Boss, dey say dey ain't going divide up no land with de niggers or give
dem no home or mule or dere freedom or nothing. Dey say dey will
wade knee-deep in blood and die first.

When de War started to break out, Master Sam enlisted in de troops
and was sent to Virginny. Dere he stay for de longest. I hear Old Miss
telling about de letters she got from him, and how he wishing dey hurry
and start de battle so's he can get through killing de Yankees and get de
War over and come home. Bless my soul, it wasn't long before dey had
de battle what Master Sam was shot in. He wrote de letter from de hospital where dey had took him. He say dey had a hard fight, dat a ball
busted his gun, and another ball shoot his accouterments off him; de
third shot tear a big hole right through de side of his neck. De doctor
done sew de wound up; he not hurt so bad. He soon be back with his
company.

But it wasn't long 'fore dey wrote some more letters to Old Miss and
say dat Master Sam's wound not getting no better; it wasn't healing to

do no good; every time dat dey sew de gash up in his neck it broke loose again. De Yankees had been putting poison grease on de bullets. Dat was de reason de wound wouldn't get well. Dey feared Master Sam was going to die, and a short time after dat letter come I sure knowed it was so. One night just about dusk dark, de screech owls dey come in a swarm and lit in de big trees in de front of de house. A mist of dust come up and de owls dey holler and carry on so dat Old Master get he gun and shot if off to scare dem away. Dat was a sign, Boss, dat somebody going to die. I just knowed it was Master Sam.

Sure enough, de next day dey got de message dat Master Sam dead. Dey brung him home all de way from Virginny and buried him in de graveyard on de other side of de garden with his gray clothes on him and de flag on de coffin. Dat's what I'se telling you, Boss, 'cause dey called all de niggers in and allowed dem to look at Master Sam. I seen him and he sure looked like he peaceful in he coffin with his soldier clothes on. I heared afterwards dat Master Sam bucked and rared just 'fore he died and tried to get out of de bed, and dat he cussed to de last.

It was this way, Boss, how come me to be in de War. You see, dey required all of de slaveowners to send so many niggers to de army to work digging de trenches and throwing up de breastworks and repairing de railroads what de Yankees done destroyed. Every master was required to send one nigger for every ten dat he had. If you had a hundred niggers, you had to send ten of dem to de army. I was one of dem dat my master's required to send. Dat was de worst times dat this here nigger ever seen, and de way dem white men drive us niggers, it was something awful. De strap, it was going from 'fore day till way after night. De niggers, heaps of dem, just fall in dey tracks give out and dem white men laying de strap on dere backs without ceasing. Dat was exactly de way it was with dem niggers like me what was in de army work. I had to stand it, Boss, till de War was over.

Dat sure was a bad war dat went on in Georgia. Dat it was. Did you ever hear about de Andersonville prison in Georgia? I tell you, Boss, dat was about de worst place dat ever I seen. Dat was where dey keep all de Yankees dat dey capture, and dey had so many dey couldn't nigh take care of dem. Dey had dem fenced up with a tall wire fence and never had enough house room for all dem Yankees. Dey would just throw de grub to dem. De most dat dey had for dem to eat was peas, and de filth, it was terrible. De sickness, it broke out 'mongst dem all de while, and dey just die like rats what been poisoned. De first thing dat de Yankees do when dey take de state away from de Confederates was to free all dem what in de prison at Andersonville.

Slavery time was tough, Boss. You just don't know how tough it was. I can't explain to you just how bad all de niggers want to get dey freedom. With de "free niggers" it was just de same as it was with dem dat was in bondage. You know dere was some few "free niggers" in dat time even 'fore de slaves taken out of bondage. It was really worse on dem dan it was with dem what wasn't free. De slaveowners, dey just despised dem "free niggers" and make it just as hard on dem as dey can. Dey couldn't get no work from nobody. Wouldn't any man hire dem or give dem any work at all. So because dey was up against it and never had any money or nothing, de white folks make dese free niggers assess de taxes. And 'cause dey never had no money for to pay dere tax with, dey was put up on de block by de court man or de sheriff and sold out to somebody for enough to pay de tax what dey say dey owe. So dey keep dese free niggers hired out all de time, most working for to pay de taxes. I remember one of dem free niggers mighty well. He was called "free Sol." He had him a little home and a old woman and some boys. Dey was kept bounded out nigh about all de time working to pay dere tax. Yes, sir, Boss, it was heap more better to be a slave nigger dan a free one. And it was really a heavenly day when de freedom come for de race.

In de time of slavery another thing what make it tough on de niggers was dem times when a man and he wife and dere children had to be taken away from one another. This separation might be brung about most any time for one thing or another—such as one or de other, de man or de wife, be sold off or taken away to some other state like Louisiana or Mississippi. Den when a master die what had a heap of slaves, these slave niggers be divided up 'mongst de master's children or sold off for to pay de master's debts. Den at times when a man married to a woman dat don't belong to de same master what he do, den dey is liable to get divided up and separated most any day. Dey was heaps of nigger families dat I know what was separated in de time of bondage dat tried to find dere folks what was gone. But de most of dem never get together again even after dey set free 'cause dey don't know where one or de other is.

After de War over and de slaves taken out of dere bondage, some of de very few white folks give dem niggers what dey liked de best: a small piece of land for to work. But de most of dem never give dem nothing, and dey sure despise dem niggers what left dem. Us old master say he wants to arrange with all his niggers to stay on with him, dat he going give dem a mule and a piece of ground. But us know dat Old Miss ain't going to agree to dat. And sure enough, she wouldn't. I'se tellin' you de truth, every nigger on dat place left. Dey sure done dat; and Old Master and Old Miss, dey never had a hand left dere on dat great big place, and all dat ground laying out.

De government seen to it dat all de white folks had to make contracts with de niggers dat stuck with dem, and dey was sure strict about dat too. De white folks at first didn't want to make de contracts and say dey wasn't going to. So de government filled de jail with dem, and after dat everyone make de contract.

When my race first got dere freedom and begin to leave dere masters, a heap of de masters got raging mad and just tore up truck. Dey say dey going to kill every nigger dey find. Some of dem did do dat very thing, Boss, sure enough. I'm telling you de truth. Dey shot niggers down by de hundreds. Dey just wasn't going let dem enjoy dey freedom. Dat is de truth, Boss.

After I come back to de old home place from working for de army, it wasn't long 'fore I left dere and get me a job with a sawmill and worked for de sawmill peoples for about five years. One day I heared some niggers telling about a white man what done come in dere getting up a big lot of niggers to take to Arkansas. Dey was telling about what a fine place it was in Arkansas, and how rich de land is, and dat de crops grow without working, and dat de 'taters grow big as a watermelon and you never have to plant dem but de one time, and all such as dat. Well, I decided to come. I joined up with de man and come to Phillips County in 1875. A heap of niggers come from Georgia at de same time dat me and Callie come. You know Callie, dat's my old woman what's in de shack dere right now. Us first lived on Mr. Jim Bush's place over close to Barton. Us ain't been far off from dere ever since us first landed in dis county. Fact is, Boss, us ain't been out of de county since us first came here, and us going to be here now, I know, 'till de Lord call for us to come on home.

FANNIE MOORE

Interviewed at Asheville, North Carolina
Interviewed by Marjorie Jones
Age when interviewed: 88

NOWADAYS WHEN I hear folks a-growlin' and a-grumblin' about not havin' this and that I just think what would they done if they be brought up on de Moore plantation. De Moore plantation belong to Marse Jim Moore, in Moore, South Carolina. De Moores had owned de same plantation and de same niggers and dey children for years back. When Marse Jim's pappy die he leave de whole thing to Marse Jim, if he take care of his mammy. She sure was a rip-jack. She say niggers didn't need nothin' to eat. Dey just like animals, not like other folks. She whip me, many time with a cowhide, till I was black and blue.

Marse Jim's wife was Mary Anderson. She was the sweetest woman I ever saw. She was always good to every nigger on de plantation. Her mother was Harriet Anderson and she visit de missus for long time on de farm. All de little niggers like to work for her. She never talk mean. Just smile dat sweet smile and talk in de softest tone. An when she laugh, she sound just like de little stream back of de spring house gurglin' past de rocks. And her hair all white and curly, I can 'member her always.

Marse Jim own de biggest plantation in de whole country. Just thousands acres of land. And de old Tiger River a-runnin' right through de middle of de plantation. On one side of de river stood de Big House, where de white folks live, and on the other side stood de quarters. De Big House was a purty thing all painted white, a-standin' in a patch of oak trees. I can't remember how many rooms in dat house but powerful many. O' course it was built when de Moores had such large families.

Marse Jim, he only had five children, not twelve like his mammy had. Dey was Andrew, and Tom, den Harriet, Nan, and Nettie Sue. Harriet was just like her Granny Anderson. She was good to everybody. She get de little niggers down and teach 'em dey Sunday school lesson.

If old Marse Jim's mammy catch her she sure raise torment. She make life just as hard for de niggers as she can.

De quarters just long row of cabins daubed with dirt. Everyone in de family live in one big room. In one end was a big fireplace. Dis had to heat de cabin and do de cookin' too. We cooked in a big pot hung on a rod over de fire and bake de corn pone in de ashes, or else put it in de skillet and cover de lid with coals. We always have plenty wood to keep us warm. Dat is if we have time to get it out of de woods.

My granny she cook for us chillens while our mammy away in de field. Dey wasn't much cookin' to do. Just make corn pone and bring in de milk. She have a big wooden bowl with enough wooden spoons to go round. She put de milk in de bowl and break it up. Den she put de bowl in de middle of de floor and all de chillen grab a spoon.

My mammy she work in de field all day and piece and quilt all night. Den she have to spin enough thread to make four cuts for de white folks every night. Why sometime I never go to bed. Have to hold de light for her to see by. She have to piece quilts for de white folks too. Why, dey is a scar on my arm yet where my brother let de pine drip on me. Rich pine was all de light we ever had. My brother was a-holdin' de pine so's I can help mammy tack the quilt and he go to sleep and let it drop.

I never see how my mammy stand such hard work. She stand up for her chillen though. De old overseer he hate my mammy, 'cause she fight him for beatin' her chillen. Why she get more whippin' for dat dan anythin' else. She have twelve chillen. I 'member I see de three oldest stand in de snow up to dey knees to split rails, while de overseer stand off and grin.

My mammy she trouble in her heart about de way they treated. Every night she pray for de Lord to get her and her chillen out of de place. One day she plowin' in de cotton field. All sudden like she let out big yell. Den she start singin' and a-shoutin' and a-whoopin' and a-hollerin'. Den it seems she plow all de harder.

When she come home, Marse Jim's mammy say: "What all dat goin' on in de field? You think we send you out there just to whoop and yell? No siree, we put you out there to work and you sure better work, else we get de overseer to cowhide you old black back."

My mammy just grin all over her black wrinkled face and say: "I'se saved. De Lord done tell me I'se saved. Now I know de Lord will show me de way, I ain't gwine to grieve no more. No matter how much you all done beat me and my chillen de Lord will show me de way. And some day we never be slaves." Old Granny Moore grab de cowhide and slash Mammy cross de back but Mammy never yell. She just go back to de field a singin'.

My mammy grieve lots over brother George, who die with de fever.

Granny she doctor him as best she could, every time she get ways from de white folks' kitchen. My mammy never get chance to see him, 'cept when she get home in de evenin'. George, he just lie. One day I look at him and he had such a peaceful look on his face, I think he sleep and just let him alone. 'Long in the evenin' I think I try to wake him. I touch him on de face, but he was dead. Mammy never know till she come at night. Poor Mammy she kneel by de bed and cry her heart out. Old Uncle Allen, he make pine box for him and carry him to de grave-yard over de hill. My mammy just plow and cry as she watch 'em put George in de ground.

My pappy he was a blacksmith. He shoe all de horses on de planta-tion. He work so hard he have no time to go to de field. His name was Stephen Moore. Marse Jim call him Stephen Andrew. He was sold to de Moores, and his mammy too. She was brought over from Africa. She never could speak plain. All her life she been a slave. White folks never recognize 'em any more dan if dey was a dog.

It was a terrible sight to see de speculators come to de plantation. Dey would go through de fields and buy de slaves dey wanted. Marse Jim never sell Pappy or Mammy or any of dey chillen. He always like Pappy. When de speculator come all de slaves start a-shakin'. No one know who is a-goin'.

Den sometimes dey take 'em and sell 'em on de block. De "breed woman" always bring more money den de rest, even de men. When dey put her on de block dey put all her chillen around her to show folks how fast she can have chillen. When she sold, her family never see her again. She never know how many chillen she have. Sometime she have colored chillen and sometimes white. 'Tain't no use to say anything, 'cause if she do she just get whipped.

Why, on de Moore plantation Aunt Cheney—everybody call her Aunt Cheney—have two chillen by de overseer. De overseer name was Hill. He was as mean as de devil. When Aunt Cheney not do what he ask he tell Granny Moore. Old Granny call Aunt Cheney to de kitchen and make her take her clothes off, den she beat her till she just black and blue. Many boys and girls marry dey own brothers and sisters and never know de difference lest they get to talkin' about dey parents and where dey used to live.

De niggers always have to get pass to go anywhere off de plantation. Dey get de pass from de massa or de missus. Den when de patterollers come dey had to show de pass to dem. If you had no pass dey strip you and beat you.

I remember one time dey was a dance at one of de houses in de quar-ters. All de niggers was a-laughin' and a-pattin' dey feet and a-singin', but dey was a few dat didn't. De patterollers shove de door open and start grabbin' us. Uncle Joe's son he decide dey was one time to die and he start to fight. He say he tired standin' so many beatin's, he just can't stand no more. De patterollers start beatin' him and he start fightin'. Oh lordy, it was terrible. Dey whip him with a cowhide for a long time, den one of dem take a stick and hit him over de head, and just bust his head wide open. De poor boy fell on de floor just a-moanin' and a-groanin'. De patterollers just whip about half dozen other niggers and send 'em home and leave us with de dead boy.

None of the niggers have any learnin', weren't never allowed to as much as pick up a piece of paper. My daddy slip and get a Webster book and den he take it out in de field and he learn to read. De white folks afraid to let de chillen learn anythin'. They afraid dey get too smart and be harder to manage. Dey never let 'em know anythin' about anythin'.

Never have any church. If you go, you set in de back of de white folks' church. But de niggers slip off and pray and hold prayer-meetin' in de woods, den dey turn down a big wash pot and prop it up with a stick to drown out de sound of de singin'. I 'member some of de songs we used to sing. One of dem went somethin' like dis:

> Hark from de tomb a doleful sound,
> My ears hear a tender cry,
> A livin' man come through the ground
> Where we may shortly lie.
> Here in dis clay may be your bed,
> In spite of all your toil,
> Let all de wise bow reverent head
> Must lie as low as ours.

Back in those times dey wasn't no way to put away fruit and things for winter like dey is today. In de fall of de year it certainly was a busy time. We peel bushels of apples and peaches to dry. Dey put up lots of brandied peaches too. De way dey done, dey peel de peaches and cut 'em up. Den dey put a layer of peaches in a crock, den a layer of sugar, den another layer of peaches until de crock was full. Den dey seal de jar by puttin' a cloth over de top, then a layer of paste, then another cloth, then another layer of paste. Dey keep dey meat about de same way folks do today 'cept dey had to smoke it more, since salt was so scarce back in dat day. Dey can most of de other fruit and put it in de same kind of jars dat dey put de peaches in. Dey string up long strings of beans and let 'em dry and cook 'em with fatback in de winter.

Folks back den never hear tell of all de ailments de folks have now. Dere were no doctors. Just use roots and bark for teas of all kinds. My old granny used to make tea out of dogwood bark and give it to us chillen when we have a cold, else she make a tea out of wild cherry bark, pennyroyal, or horehound. My goodness but dey was bitter. We do most anything to get out of takin' de tea, but 'twarn't no use. Granny just get you by de collar, hold your nose, and you just swallow it or get strangled. When de baby have de colic she gets rats vein and make a syrup and put a little sugar in it and boil it. Den soon as it cold she give it to de baby. For stomachache she give us snake root. Sometime she make tea, other time she just cut it up in little pieces and make you eat one or two of dem. When you have fever she wrap you up in cabbage leaves or ginseng leaves. Dis make de fever go. When de fever got too bad, she take the hoofs off de hog dat had been killed and parch 'em in de ashes and den she beat 'em up and make a tea. Dis was de most terrible of all.

De year before de War started Marse Jim died. He was out in de pasture pickin' up cow loads, a-throwin' 'em in de garden. And he just drop over. I hate to see Marse Jim go, he not such a bad man. After he die his boys, Tom and Andrew, take charge of de plantation. Dey think dey run things different from dey daddy, but dey just get started when de War come. Marse Tom and Marse Andrew both have to go. My pappy he go along with dem to do dere cookin'. My pappy he say dat some day he run four or five miles with de Yankees behind him before he can stop to do any cookin'. Den when he stop he cook with de bullets a fallin' all round de kettles. He say he walk on dead men just like he walkin' on de ground. Some of de men be dead, some moanin' and some a-groanin', but nobody pay no attention, 'cause de Yankees keep a-comin'.

One day de Yankees come awful close. Marse Andrew have de Confederate flag in his hand. He raise it high in de air. Pappy say he yell for him to put de flag down 'cause de Yankees was a-comin' closer and was a-goin' to capture him anyway. But Marse Andrew just hold de flag up and run behind a tree. De Yankee soldiers just take one shot at him and dat was de last of him. My pappy bring him home. De family put him in alcohol. One day I went to see him and there he was a-swimmin' round in de water. Most of his hair done come off, through. He buried at Nazareth. I could go right back to de graveyard if I was there.

Den my pappy go back to stay with Marse Tom. Marse Tom was just wounded. If he hadn't had a Bible in his pocket de bullet go clear through his heart. But you all know no bullet ain't goin' through de Bible. No, you can't shoot through God's word. Pappy he bring Marse Tom home and take care of him till he well. Marse Tom give Pappy a horse and wagon 'cause he say he save his life.

Many time de soldiers come through de plantation and dey load up dey wagons with everything dey find, 'lasses, hams, chickens. Sometime dey give part of it to de niggers but de white folks take it away when dey get gone. De white folks hide all de silverware from de soldiers. Dey afraid dey take it when dey come. Sometimes dey make us tell if dey think we know.

After de War Pappy go back to work on de plantation. He make his own crop on de plantation. But de money was no good den. I played with many a Confederate dollar. He sure was happy dat he was free. Mammy, she shout for joy and say her prayers were answered. Pappy get pretty feeble, but he work till just before he die. He made patch of cotton with a hoe. Dey was enough cotton in de patch to make a bale. Pappy die when he 104 years old. Mammy she lived to be 105.

After de War de Ku Klux broke out. Oh, dey was mean! In dey long white robes dey scare de niggers to death. Dey keep close watch on dem, afraid dey try to do somethin'. Dey have long horns and big eyes and mouth. Dey never go round much in de day. Just night. Dey take de poor niggers away in de woods and beat 'em and hang 'em. De niggers was afraid to move, much less try to do anything. Dey never know what to do, dey have no learnin'. Have no money. All dey can do was stay on de same plantation till dey can do better. We live on de same plantation till de chillen all grown and Mammy and Pappy both die. Then we leave. I don't know where any of my people are now. I knows I was born in 1849. I was eighty-eight years old de first of September.

WILLIAM MOORE

Interviewed in Dallas, Texas
Interviewed by Heloise M. Foreman
Age when interviewed: 83

MY MAMMY told me that the reason why her and my pa's name am Moore was because afore they belonged to Marse Tom Waller, they belonged to Marse Moore, but he sold 'em off.

Marse Tom heared they gwine emancipate the slaves in Selma, so he got his things and niggers together and come to Texas. My mammy said they come in covered wagons but I wasn't old enough to remember nothin' 'bout it. The first 'lections I got is down in Limestone County [Texas].

Marse Tom had a fine, big house painted white and a big prairie field front his house and two, three farms and orchards. He had five hundred head of sheep, and I spent most my time bein' a shepherd boy. I starts out when I'm little and learns right fast to keep good 'count of the sheeps.

Mammy's name was Jane and pa's was Ray, and I had a brother, Ed, and four sisters—Rachel and Mandy and Harriet and Ellen. We had a purty hard time to make out and was hungry lots of times. Marse Tom didn't feel called on to feed his hands any too much. I remembers I had a cravin' for victuals all the time. My mammy used to say, "My belly craves somethin' and it craves meat." I'd take lunches to the field hands and they'd say, "Lord God, it ain't 'nough to stop the gripe in you belly." We made out on things from the fields and rabbits cooked in little fires.

We had little bitty cabins out of logs with puncheon beds and a bench and fireplace in it. We chillen made out to sleep on pallets on the floor.

Some Sundays we went to church someplace. We always liked to go anyplace. A white preacher always told us to obey our masters and work hard and sing and when we die we go to Heaven. Marse Tom didn't mind us singin' in our cabins at night, but we better not let him catch us prayin'. Seems like niggers just got to pray. Half they life am in

94

prayin'. Some nigger take turn 'bout to watch and see if Marse Tom always 'bout, then they circle theyselves on the floor in the cabin and pray. They get to moanin' low and gentle. "Some day, some day, some day, this yoke gwine be lifted off our shoulders."

Marse Tom been dead long time now. I believe he's in hell. Seem like that where he belong. He was a terrible mean man and had a indifferent, mean wife. But he had the finest, sweetest chillen the Lord ever let live and breathe on this earth. They's so kind and sorrowin' over us slaves. Some them chillen used to read us little things out of papers and books. We'd look at them papers and books like they somethin' mighty curious, but we better not let Marse Tom or his wife know it!

Marse Tom was a fitty man for meanness. He just 'bout had to beat somebody every day to satisfy his cravin'. He had a big bullwhip, and he stake a nigger on the ground and make 'nother nigger hold his head down with his mouth in the dirt and whip the nigger till the blood run out and red up the ground. We little niggers stand round and see it done. Then he tell us, "Run to the kitchen and get some salt from Jane." That my mammy, she was cook. He's sprinkle salt in the cut-open places and the skin jerk and quiver and the man slobber and puke. Then his shirt stick to his back for a week or more.

My mammy had a terrible bad back once. I seen her tryin' to get the clothes off her back and a woman say, "What's the matter with you back?" It was raw and bloody, and she say Marse Tom done beat her with a handsaw with the teeth to her back. She died with the marks on her, the teeth holes goin' crosswise her back. When I'se growed I asks her 'bout it, and she say Marse Tom got mad at the cookin' and grabs her by the hair and drug her out the house and grabs the saw off the tool bench and whips her.

My pa is the first picture I got in my mind. I was settin' on Ma's lap and Pa come in and say Marse Tom loaned him out to work on a dam they's buildin' in Houston and he has to go. One day word come he was haulin' a load of rocks through the swamps and a low-hangin' grape-vine catched him under the neck and jerked him off the seat and the wagon rolled over him and kilt him dead. They buried him down there somewheres.

One day I'm down in the hog pen and hears a loud agony screamin' up to the house. When I got up close I see Marse Tom got Mammy tied to a tree with her clothes pulled down, and he's layin' it on her with the bullwhip, and the blood am runnin' down her eyes and off her back. I goes crazy. I say, "Stop, Marse Tom," and he swings the whip and don't reach me good, but it cuts just the same. I sees Miss Mary standin' in the cookhouse door. I runs 'round crazy like and sees a big rock, and I takes it and throws it, and it catches Marse Tom in the skull and he goes down like a poled ox. Miss Mary comes out and lifts her pa and helps him in the house and then comes and helps me undo Mammy. Mammy and me takes to the woods for two, three months, I guess. My sisters meets us and grease Mammy's back and brings us victuals. Purty soon they say it am safe for us to come in the cabin to eat at night and they watch for Marse Tom.

One day Marse Tom's wife am in the yard and she calls me and say she got somethin' for me. She keeps her hand under her apron. She keeps beggin' me to come up to her. She say, "Gimme you hand." I reaches out my hand and she grabs it and slips a slip-knot rope over it. I sees then that's what she had under her apron and the other end was tied to a little bush. I tries to get loose and runs 'round, and I trips her and she falls and breaks her arm. I gets the rope off my arm and runs.

Mammy and me stays hid in the brush then. We sees Sam and Billie, and they tell us they am fightin' over us niggers. Then they done told us the niggers declared to Marse Tom they ain't gwine be no more beatin's and we could come up and stay in our cabin and they'd see Marse Tom didn't do nothin'. And that's what Mammy and me did. Sam and Billie was two the biggest niggers on the place, and they done got the shotguns out of the house some way or another. One day Marse Tom am in a rocker on the porch and Sam and Billie am standin' by with the guns. We all seen five white men ridin' up. When they gets near, Sam say to Marse Tom, "First white man sets his self inside that rail fence gets it from the gun." Marse Tom waves the white men to go back, but they gallops right up to the fence and swings off they hosses.

Marse Tom say, "Stay outside, gentlemen, please do, I done change my mind." They say, "What's the matter here? We come to whip you niggers like you done hire us to."

Marse Tom say, "I done change my mind, but if you stay outside I'll bring you the money." They argues to come in but Marse Tom outtalk them and they say they'll go if he brings them they three dollars apiece. He takes them the money and they goes away. Marse Tom cuss and rare, but the niggers just stay in the woods and fool 'way they time. They say it ain't no use to work for nothin' all them days.

One day I'm in a 'simmon tree in the middle of a little pond, eatin' 'simmons, and my sister, Mandy, come runnin'. She say, "Us niggers am free." I looks over to the house and seen the niggers pilin' they little bunch of clothes and things outside they cabins. Then Mammy come runnin' with some other niggers, and Mammy was head runner. I clumb down out that tree and run to meet her. She say Marse Tom done told her he gwine keep me and pay her for it. She's a-scared I'll stay if I wants to or not and she begs me not to.

We gets up to the house and all the niggers standin' there with they little bundles on they head and they all say, "Where we goin'?"

Mammy said, "I don't know where you all goin' but me, myself, am goin' to go to Miss Mary." So all the niggers gets in the cart with Mammy, and we goes to Miss Mary. She meets us by the back door and say, "Come in, Jane, and all you chillen and all the rest of you. You can see my door am open and my smokehouse door am open to you, and I'll bed you down till we figurates a way for you." We all cries and sings and prays and was so excited we didn't eat no supper, though Mammy stirs up some victuals.

It warn't long afore we found places to work. Miss Mary found us a place with a fine white man, and we works on sharance and drifts round to some other places and lives in Corsicana for a while and buys Mammy a little house and she died there.

I got married and had three chillen—cute, fetchin' little chillen—and they went to school. Wasn't no trouble 'bout school then, but was when Emancipation come. My brother Ed was in school then and the Ku Klux come and drove the Yankee lady and gentleman out and closed the school.

My chillen growed up and my wife died, and I spent most my days workin' hard on farms. Now I'm old and throwed away. But I'm thankful to God and praiseful for the pension what lets me have a little somethin' to eat and a place to stay.

ANDREW MOSS

Interviewed at Knoxville, Tennessee
Interviewer not identified
Age when interviewed: 85

ONE THING dat's all wrong with dis world today is dat dey ain't no "prayer grounds." Down in Georgia where I was born—dat way back in 1852—us colored folks had prayer grounds. My mammy's was a old twisted thick-rooted muscadine bush. She'd go in dere and pray for deliverance of de slaves. Some colored folks cleaned out knee-spots in de canebrakes. Cane, you know, grows high and thick, and colored folks could hide demselves dere and nobody could see and pester dem.

You see it was just like dis. Durin' de War, and before de War too, white folks make a heap o' fun of de colored folks for all time prayin'. Sometime, say, you was a slave and you get down to pray in de field or by de side of de road and Marster come along and see a slave on his knees. He say, "What you prayin' about?" And you say, "Oh, Marster, I'se just prayin' to Jesus 'cause I wants to go to Heaven when I dies." And Marster says, "You's my Negro. I get ye to Heaven. Get up offen your knees." De white folks what owned slaves thought that when dey go to Heaven de colored folks would be dere to wait on 'em.

And if it was a Yank come along, he say too, "What you prayin' about?" You gives de same response. And he say, "We's gwine save you. We goin' to set you free. You wants to be free, don't you?" "Yes sir, Boss!" "Well den," Yank say, "come go along with me." Ain't no use keep sayin', "Please, sir, Boss. I'll have to ask my marster." Yank say, "What you mean, Marster? You ain't got no marster. We's settin' you free."

Sometimes dey takes and tie a rope round you, and they starts ridin' off, but dey don't go too fast so you walk behind. Sometimes along comes another Yank on a horse and he ask, "Boy, ain't you tired?" "Yes sir, Boss!" "Well, you get up here behind me and ride some." Den he wrap de rope all round de saddle horn. Wraps and wraps, but leaves some slack. But he keeps you tied, so's you won't jump down and run away. And many's de time a prayin' Negro got took off like dat and weren't never seen no more.

Course, if you goes with 'em, you 'member your trainin' and before you leaves de field, you stacks your hoe nice, like you was quittin' de day's work. Dey learned de little 'uns to do dat, soon's dey begins to work in de fields. Dey had little hoes, handles about de size of my arm, for de little fellers. I've walked many a mile, when I was a little feller, up and down de rows, followin' de grown folks, and chopping with de hoe round de corners where de earth was soft so de little 'uns could hoe easy.

Whoopee! Let dat dinner horn blow, and everybody stacks dey hoes, nice, neat stack standin' up, and starts to run. Some eats in dey own cabins, but dem what eats at de Big House sets down at a long table and gets good grub too. Every night our marster give us every one a glass o' whiskey. Dat's to keep off disease. Mornin's we had to all drink tar water for de same purpose. Dat wasn't so tasty.

My marster's name was George Hopper. Dat man paid taxes on more'n two thousand acres of land in two counties. I lived in dem two counties, was born in Wilkes and raised in Lincoln county, Georgia. We called it de middle south. My marster he never did marry. Lots of folks didn't; dey just took up with one another. Marster Hopper had five children by my grandmother. She was his house woman; dat's what he call her. And when he died he willed her and all dem chillens a house, some land, and a little money. He'd of left 'em a heap more money and he'd been one of the richest men in the county, if de War hadn't broke out.

When it was over he had a barrel full of 'Federate greenbacks. But 'tweren't no count. He done broke den. One day my uncle—he was the colored overseer—he went to Danbury, six miles from where we lived at, and he paid five dollars a pound for coffee. Dat was before de North whipped de South, and dey hadn't killed down de money value for de South.

Talk about hard times! We seed 'em in dem days, durin' de War and most 'specially after de surrender. Folks dese days don't know what trouble looks like. We was glad to eat ash cakes and drink parched corn and rye 'stead o' coffee. I'se seed my grandmother go to de smokehouse and scrape up de dirt where de meat had dropped off and take it to de house for seasonin'. You see, both armies fed off de white folks, and dey cleaned out dey barns and cellars and smokehouses when dey come. One time when de Yanks was on de way to Augusta, I was picking up chips to make the supper fire, when I seed 'em comin'. I hit it out from dere and hide behind two little hills down by de big spring. After a while my brother find me and he tell me to come on back to the house and see dem white mens dance. De Yanks kept comin' and dey eat all night. By daylight dey was through marchin' past.

And den come de Rebels. When dey come we had five thousand bushel of corn, one hundred head o' hogs, three hundred and fifty gallons o' syrup and such. When dey left, dey took and set fire to everything, to keep it away from the Yanks, aimin' to starve 'em out o' dat country. Dat's what dey done. Some of dem Rebels was mean as the Yanks. And dat was bein' mean! Some called de Yanks, "de Hornets," 'cause dey fight so. Take a Yank and he'd fight across a buzz saw and it circlin' fifty mile a minute.

Dat time when the Yanks was goin' to Augusta, and I went to black my marster's boots—he'd give us a two-cent piece, big as a quarter, for boot blackin'—I say, "Marster, who is dem soldiers?" And he say to me, "Dey is de Yankees come to try to take you away from me." And I say, "Looks like to me, Marster, if dey wants to take us dey'd ask you for us." Marster laughed and say, "Boy! Dem fellers don't ask with words. Dey does all they talkin' with cannons."

Did you know that a white woman shot de first cannon dat was ever fired in de state of Georgia? She was a Yankee colonel's wife, dey say, named Miss Anna. I dunno the rest of her name. She wants to be de first to fire a cannon, she say, to set de Negroes free. Dat was before de War begin. De roar of dat cannon was in folk's ears for more'n five days and nights.

How I come to Knoxville—I was a young man when I started off from Georgia, aimin' to go over de mountains to Kentucky where I heard dey pay good wages. I stopped in Campbell County, Tennessee, with another feller, and I seed a pretty gal workin' in de field, and I says, "I'm goin' to marry dat gal." Sure 'nough me and her was married in less dan six months. Her marster built us a log house and we lived there till we come to Knoxville, Tennessee. Now all of my boys is dead. Every one of 'em worked for Mr. Peters, of Peters and Bradley Flour Mills, and dey all died workin' for him. So Mister Willie, he say he gwine let me live here, in de company house, the rest o' my days.

DELICIA PATTERSON

Interviewed at St. Louis, Missouri
Interviewer not identified
Age when interviewed: 92

I WAS born in Boonville, Missouri, January 2, 1845. My mother's name was Maria and my father's was Jack Wiley. Mother had five children but raised only two of us. I was owned by Charles Mitchell until I was fifteen years old. They were fairly nice to all of their slaves and they had several of us.

I only got whipped once in the whole fifteen years there, and that was because I was working in the garden with one of my owner's daughters and I pulled up something that she did not want pulled up, so she up and slapped me for it. I got so mad at her, I taken up a hoe and run her all the way in the Big House, and of course I got whipped for that.

I did not even have to sleep in the cabins. I slept on a pallet in the bedrooms with Old Marse's children. I was a pet anywhere I worked, because I was always very neat and clean, and a good worker.

When I was fifteen years old, I was brought to the courthouse, put up on the auction block to be sold. Old Judge Miller from my county was there. I knew him well because he was one of the wealthiest slave owners in the county, and the meanest one. He was so cruel all the slaves and many owners hated him because of it. He saw me on the block for sale, and he knew I was a good worker. So, when he bid for me, I spoke right out on the auction block and told him: "Old Judge Miller don't you bid for me, 'cause if you do, I would not live on your plantation. I will take a knife and cut my own throat from ear to ear before I would be owned by you."

So he stepped back and let someone else bid for me. My own father knew I was to be for sale, so he brought his owner to the sale for him to buy me, so we could be together. But when father's owner heard what I said to Judge Miller, he told my father he would not buy me, because I was sassy, and he never owned a sassy nigger and did not want one that was sassy. That broke my father's heart, but I couldn't help that. Another nigger trader standing right beside my father's owner said, "I wouldn't own a nigger that didn't have some spunk." So I was sold to a Southern Englishman named Thomas Steele for fifteen hundred dollars. He had an old slave he had in his home for years as their housekeeper, and his wife did not like her, and he had to sell her to keep peace at home. So he put me in his buggy and taken me home to his wife and told her, "I bought you another girl, Susianna, but I don't want you to lay the weight of your finger on her when she disobeys. Let me know and I will punish her myself."

I lived in that family until after the Civil War was over. Mr. Steele's wife's people had a big family and they visited the Steeles a great deal. Mr. Tom didn't like them because they were Yankees and the Steeles were Confederates. So one time Mr. Tom was going away on a trip and he knew, when he was gone, his wife would have all her folks in the home visiting, and that was against his wishes. He told me to keep tab on every time her relatives came to the house and how long they stayed, and tell him when he come back home, and that he would leave orders in the home to let me work in the field, so I would not have to bother with that great big family. When he left, all his wife's folks come right down on our plantation, so I had to work in the house for them so hard. I did not have time to even look at the field.

When my old boss come home I told him I had not worked in the field and why. Him and his wife had a big fight about that, and she hated me for a long time, and said the idea of her husband taking a nigger's word to hers and mistreat her on account of it. But he did not let her bother me about nothing, so I stayed on with them until one day, while I had a fly brush in my hand fanning flies while they ate, she told him something I done she didn't like. Just to please her, he taken the fly brush out of my hand and just tapped me with it. It didn't hurt me a bit, but it made me so mad I just went straight to the kitchen, left all the dishes, put on my sunbonnet and run away.

I stayed two weeks. He sent everybody he thought knew where I was after me, and told them to tell me if I would only come on back home, no one would ever bother me anymore. I hid in the woods two weeks and was not afraid. I would be afraid out in those woods now, but I wasn't then. At night I would come up to some of the slave cabins who were my friends and eat and stay all night. So I went back home after my two weeks off as a runaway nigger and no one ever bothered me anymore either. I came to St. Louis with them, during the Civil War.

When freedom was declared Mr. Steele told me that I was as free as he was. He said I could leave them if I please or could stay, that they wanted me and would be glad to have me if I would stay, and his wife said, "'Course she is our nigger. She is as much our nigger now as she was the day you bought her two years ago and paid fifteen hundred dollars for her."

That made me mad so I left right then, since she was so smart. Her husband told her, "Now, Sue, you might as well face it. There are no more slaves and won't ever be any more, regardless of how much we paid for them. So just quiet yourself down. She don't have to stay here if she don't want to." Till this day some of their children come to visit me, but they never give me anything ever.

I hired myself out to a family named Miller at three dollars a week, and lived on the place. I had a baby about three years old. I married before the War and when my baby was two weeks old they taken my husband in the army. He died in the army. I worked for the Millers about eleven months. One day Mrs. Miller misplaced her silver thimble and she accused me of stealing it. She did not tell me that but she told the white nurse girl, and the nurse told me. I got so mad at her for that 'cause I never stole anything in my whole life and never been accused of stealing, so I quit. They begged me to stay and offered to raise my salary, but I told them I would not work for anyone who felt I would steal. The very next day she found her thimble in the nursery where she remembered she put it herself, but forgot about it at the time. She thought it was lost.

I don't know what the ex-slaves expected, but I do know they didn't get anything. After the War we just wandered from place to place, working for food and a place to stay. Now and then we got a little money, but a very little. I only voted once in my life and that was when working for Mr. Gerhart. He was a real-estate dealer and he taken me to the polls and showed me how to vote for a Republican president. It has been so long ago I don't even remember who the President was, but I do know he got elected. I think the time will soon be when people won't be looked on as regards to whether you are black or white, but all on the same equality. I may not live to see it but it is on the way. Many don't believe it, but I know it.

MARY REYNOLDS

Interviewed at Dallas, Texas
Interviewer not identified
Age when interviewed: 100⁺

MY PAW'S name was Tom Vaughn and he was from the north, born free man and lived and died free to the end of his days. He wasn't no educated man, but he was what he calls himself a piano man. He told me once he lived in New York and Chicago, and he built the insides of pianos and knew how to make them play in tune. He said some white folks from the south told he if he'd come with them to the south he'd find a lot of work to do with pianos in them parts, and he come off with them.

He saw my maw on the Kilpatrick place and her man was dead. He told Dr. Kilpatrick, my master, he'd buy my maw and her three chillen with all the money he had, if he'd sell her. But Dr. Kilpatrick was never one to sell any but the old niggers who was past workin' in the fields and past their breedin' times. So my paw marries my maw and works the fields, same as any other nigger. They had six gals: Martha and Pamela and Josephine and Ellen and Katherine and me.

I was born same time as Miss Sara Kilpatrick. Dr. Kilpatrick's first wife and my maw come to their time right together. Miss Sara's maw died and they brung Miss Sara to suck with me. It's a thing we ain't never forgot. My maw's name was Sallie, and Miss Sara always looked with kindness on my maw. We sucked till we was a fair size and played together, which wasn't no common thing. None the other little niggers played with white chillen. But Miss Sara loved me so good.

I was just about big enough to start playin' with a broom to go about sweepin' up and not even half doin' it when Dr. Kilpatrick sold me. They was a old white man in Trinity, and his wife died and he didn't have chick or child or slave or nothin'. Master sold me cheap, 'cause he didn't want Miss Sara to play with no nigger young'un. That old man bought me a big doll and went off and left me all day, with the door open. I just sat on the floor and played with that doll. I used to cry.

He'd come home and give me somethin' to eat and then go to bed, and I slept on the foot of the bed with him. I was scared all the time in the dark. He never did close the door.

Miss Sarah pined and sickened. Master done what he could, but there wasn't no pertness in her. She got sicker and sicker, and Master brung another doctor. He say, "You little gal is grievin' the life out her body and she sure goin' die if you don't do somethin' about it." Miss Sara says over and over, "I wants Mary." Master say to the doctor, "That a little nigger young'un I done sold." The doctor tells him he better get me back if he wants to save the life of his child. Dr. Kilpatrick has to give a big plenty more to get me back than what he sold me for, but Miss Sara plumps up right off and grows into fine health.

The Master marries a rich lady from Mississippi, and they has chillen for company to Miss Sara and seems like for a time she forgets me.

Massa Kilpatrick wasn't no piddlin' man. He was a man of plenty. He had a big house with no more style to it than a crib, but it could room plenty of people. He was a medicine doctor, and they was rooms in the second story for sick folks what came to lay in. It would take two days to go all over the land he owned. He had cattle and stock and sheep and more than a hundred slaves and more besides. He bought the best of niggers near every time the speculators came that way. He'd make a swap of the old ones and give money for young ones what could work.

He raised corn and cotton and cane and 'taters and goobers, besides the peas and other feedin' for the niggers. I remember I held a hoe handle mighty unsteady when they put an old woman to learn me and some other chillen to scrape the fields. That old woman would be in a frantic. She'd show me and then turn about to show some other little nigger, and I'd have the young corn cut clean as the grass. She say, "For the love of God, you better learn it right, or Solomon will beat the breath out of your body." Old man Solomon was the nigger driver.

Slavery was the worst days was ever seed in the world. They was things past tellin', but I got the scars on my old body to show to this day. I seed worse than what happened to me. I seed them put the men and women in the stock with they hands screwed down through holes in the board and they feets tied together and they naked behinds to the world. Solomon, the overseer, beat them with a big whip and Master looked on. The niggers better not stop in the fields when they hear them yellin'. They cut the flesh most to the bones, and when they taken some of them out of stock and put them on the beds, they never got up again.

When a nigger died they let his folks come out the fields to see him before he died. They buried him the same day, take a big plank and bust it with a ax in the middle enough to bend it back, and put the dead nigger in betwixt it. They'd cart them down to the graveyard on the place and not bury them deep enough that buzzards wouldn't come circlin' 'round. Niggers mourns now, but in them days they wasn't no time for mournin'.

The conch shell blowed afore daylight, and all hands better get out for roll call or Solomon bust the door down and get them out. It was work hard, get beatings and half fed. They brung the victuals and water to the fields on a slide pulled by a old mule. Plenty of times they was only a half barrel water and it stale and hot, for all us niggers on the hottest days. Mostly we ate pickled pork and corn bread and peas and beans and 'taters. They never was as much as we needed.

The time I hated most was pickin' cotton when the frost was on the bolls. My hands get sore and crack open and bleed. We'd have a little fire in the fields, and if the ones with tender hands couldn't stand it no longer, we'd run and warm our hands a little bit. When I could steal a 'tater, I used to slip it in the ashes, and when I'd run to the fire I'd take it out and eat it on the sly.

In the cabins it was nice and warm. They was built of pine boardin' and they was one long row of them up the hill back of the big house. Near one side of the cabins was a fireplace. They'd bring in two, three big logs and put on the fire and they'd last near a week. The beds was made out of puncheons fitted in holes bored in the wall, and planks laid across them poles. We had tickin' mattresses filled with corn shucks. Sometimes the men built chairs at night. We didn't know much about havin' nothin', though.

Sometimes Master let niggers have a li'l patch. They'd raise 'taters or goobers. They liked to have them to help fill out on the victuals. 'Taters roasted in the ashes was the best tastin' eatin' I ever had. I could die better satisfied to have just one more 'tater roasted in hot ashes. The niggers had to work the patches at night and dig the 'taters and goobers at night. Then if they wanted to sell any in town they'd have to get a pass to go. They had to go at night, 'cause they couldn't ever spare a hand from the fields.

Once in a while they'd give us a little piece of Saturday evenin' to wash out clothes in the branch. We hanged them on the ground in the woods to dry. They was a place to wash clothes from the well, but they was so many niggers all couldn't get round to it on Sundays. When they'd get through with the clothes on Saturday evenings, the niggers which sold they goobers and 'taters brung fiddles and guitars and come out and play. The others clap they hands and stomp they feet, and we young'uns cut a step round, I was plenty biggity and liked to cut a step.

We was scart of Solomon and his whip, though, and he didn't like frolickin'. He didn't like for us niggers to pray, either. We never heard of no church, but us have prayin' in the cabins. We'd set on the floor and pray with our heads down low and sing low, but if Solomon heared he'd come and beat on the wall with the stock of his whip. He'd say, "I'll come in there and tear the hide off you backs." But some the old niggers tell us we got to pray to God that he don't think different of the blacks and the whites. I know that Solomon is burnin' in hell today, and it pleasures me to know it.

Once my maw and paw taken me and Katherine after night to slip to another place to a prayin' and singin'. A nigger man with white beard told us a day am comin' when niggers only be slaves of God. We prays for the end of Tribulation and the end of beatings and for shoes that fit our feet. We prayed that us niggers could have all we wanted to eat and special for fresh meat. Some the old ones say we have to bear all, 'cause that all we can do. Some say they was glad to the time they's dead, 'cause they'd rather rot in the ground than have the beatin's. What I hated most was when they'd beat me and I didn't know what they beat me for, and I hated them strippin' me naked as the day I was born.

When we's comin' back from that prayin', I thought I heared the nigger dogs and somebody on horseback. I say, "Maw, it's them nigger hounds and they'll eat us up." You could hear them old hounds and sluts abayin'. Maw listens and says, "Sure enough, them dogs am runnin' and God help us!" Then she and Paw talk, and they take us to a fence corner and stands us up against the rails and say, "Don't move, and if anyone comes near, don't breathe loud." They went to the woods, so the hounds chase them and not get us. Me and Katherine stand there, holdin' hands, shakin' so we can hardly stand. We hears the hounds come nearer, but we don't move. They goes after Paw and Maw, but they circle round to the cabins and gets in. Maw say it's the power of God.

In them days I weared shirts, like all young'uns. They had collars and come below the knees and was split up the sides. That's all we weared in hot weather. The men weared jeans and the women gingham. Shoes was the worstest trouble. We weared rough russets when it got cold, and it seem powerful strange they'd never get them to fit. Once when I was a young gal, they got me a new pair and all brass studs in the toes. They was too little for me, but I had to wear them. The brass trimmin's cut into my ankles and them places got miserable bad. I rubs tallow in them sore places and wraps rags round them, and my sores got worser and worser. The scars are there to this day.

I wasn't sick much, though. Some of the niggers had chills and fever a lot, but they hadn't discovered so many diseases then as now. Dr. Kilpatrick give sick niggers ipecac and asafetida and oil and turpentine and black fever pills.

They was a cabin called the spinnin' house and two looms and two spinnin' wheels goin' all the time, and two nigger women sewin' all the time. It took plenty sewin' to make all the things for a place so big. Once Master goes to Baton Rouge and brung back a yellow gal dressed in fine style. She was a seamster nigger. He builds her a house away from the quarters, and she done fine sewin' for the whites. Us niggers knowed the doctor took a black woman quick as he did a white and took any on his place he wanted, and he took them often. But mostly the chillen born on the place looked like niggers. Aunt Cheney always say four of hers was Master's, but he didn't give them no mind. But this yellow gal breeds so fast and gets a mess of white young'uns. She learned them fine manners and combs out they hair.

Once two of them goes down the hill to the dollhouse where the Kilpatrick chillen am playin'. They wants to go in the dollhouse and one of the Kilpatrick boys say, "That's for white chillen." They say, "We ain't no niggers, 'cause we got the same daddy you has, and he comes to see us near every day and fetches us clothes and things from town." They is fussin' and Missy Kilpatrick is listenin' out her chamber window. She heard them white niggers say, "He is our daddy, and we call him Daddy when he comes to our house to see our mamma."

When Master come home that evenin' his wife hardly say nothin' to him, and he ask her what the matter and she tells him, "Since you asks me, I'm studyin' in my mind about them white young'uns of that yellow nigger wench from Baton Rouge." He say, "Now, honey, I fetches that gal just for you, 'cause she a fine seamster." She say, "It look kind of funny they got the same kind of hair and eyes as my chillen and they got a nose looks like yours." He say, "Honey, you just payin' attention to talk of little chillen that ain't got no mind to what they say." She say, "Over in Mississippi I got a home and plenty with my daddy, and I got that in my mind."

Well, she didn't never leave and Master bought her a fine new span of surrey hosses. But she don't never have no more chillen and she ain't so cordial with the master. Margaret, that yellow gal, has more white young'uns, but they don't never go down the hill no more to the Big House.

Aunt Cheney was just out of bed with a sucklin' baby one time, and she ran away. Some say that was another baby of Master's breedin'. She don't come to the house to nurse her baby, so they misses her, and old Solomon gets the nigger hounds and takes her trail. They get near her and she grabs a limb and tries to hoist herself in a tree, but them dogs grab her and pull her down. The men hollers them onto her, and the dogs tore her naked and ate the breasts plumb off her body. She got well and lived to be an old woman, but another woman has to suck her baby, and she ain't got no sign of breasts no more.

They give all the niggers fresh meat on Christmas and a plug of tobacco all around. The highest cottonpicker gets a suit of clothes and all the women what had twins that year gets an outfit of clothes for the twins and a double-warm blanket.

Seems like after I got bigger, I remember more and more niggers run away. They's most always catched. Master used to hire out his niggers for wage hands. One time he hired me and a nigger boy, Turner, to work for some ornery white trash name of Kidd. One day Turner goes off and don't come back. Old man Kidd say I knowed about it, and he tied my wrists together and stripped me. He hanged me by the wrists from a limb on a tree and spraddled my legs round the trunk and tied my feet together. Then he beat me. He beat me worser than I ever been beat before, and I faints dead away. When I come to I'm in bed. I didn't care so much if I died.

I didn't know about the passin' of time, but Miss Sara came to see me. Some white folks done get word to her. Mr. Kidd tries to talk hisself out of it, but Miss Sara fetches me home when I'm well enough to move. She took me in a cart and my maw takes care of me. Master looks me over good and says I'll get well, but I'm ruined for breedin' chillen.

After a while I take a notion to marry, and Massa and Missy marries us, same as all the niggers. They stands inside the house with a broom held crosswise of the door, and we stands outside. Missy puts a little wreath on my head they kept there, and we steps over the broom into the house. Now, that's all they was to the marryin'. After freedom I gets married and has it put in the book by the preacher.

One day we was workin' in the fields and hears the conch shell blow, so we all goes to the back gate of the Big House. Master am there. He say, "Call the roll for every nigger big 'nough to walk, and I wants them to go to the river and wait there. There's goin' to be a show and I wants you to see it." They was a big boat down there, done built up on the sides with boards and holes in the boards and a big gun barrel stickin' through every hole. We ain't never seen nothin' like that. Massa goes up the plank onto the boat and comes out on the boat porch. He say, "This am a Yankee boat." He goes inside and the water wheels starts movin', and that boat goes movin' up the river and they says it goes to Natchez.

The boat wasn't more than out of sight when a big drove of soldiers comes into town. They say they's Federals. More than half the niggers goes off with them soldiers, but I goes on back home 'cause of my old mammy.

Next day them Yankees is swarmin' the place. Some the niggers wants to show them somethin'. I follows to the woods. The niggers shows them soldiers a big pit in the ground, bigger'n a big house. It has got wooden doors that lifts up, but the top am sodded and grass growin' on it, so you couldn't tell it. In the pit is stock, horses and cows and mules and money and chinaware and silver and a mess of stuff them soldiers takes.

We just set on the place doin' nothin' till the white folks comes home. Miss Sara come out to the cabin and say she wants to read a letter to my mammy. It comes from Louis Carter, which is a brother to my mammy, and he done follow the Federals to Galveston. A white man done write the letter for him. It am tored in half and Master done that. The letter say Louis am workin' in Galveston and wants Mammy to come with us, and he'll pay our way. Miss Sara say Master swear, "Damn Louis Carter. I ain't goin' to tell Sallie nothin'," and he starts to tear the letter up. But she won't let him, and she reads it to Mammy.

After a time Master takes all his niggers what wants to Texas with him, and Mammy gets to Galveston and dies there. I goes with Master to the Tennessee Colony and then to Navasota. Miss Sara marries Mr. T. Coleman and goes to El Paso. She wrote and told me to come to her and I always meant to go.

My husband and me farmed round for times, and then I done housework and cookin' for many years. I come to Dallas and cooked seven years for one white family. My husband died years ago. I guess Miss Sara been dead these long years. I always kept my years by Miss Sara's years, 'count we is born so close.

I been blind and almost helpless for five years. I'm gettin' mighty enfeeblin', and I ain't walked outside the door for a long time back. I sets and remembers the times in the world. I remembers now clear as yesterday things I forgot for a long time. I remembers about the days of slavery, and I don't believe they ever goin' to have slaves no more on this earth. I think God done took that burden off his black chillen, and I'm aimin' to praise him for it to his face in the days of Glory, what ain't so far off.

HARRIETT ROBINSON

Interviewed at Oklahoma City, Oklahoma
Interviewer not identified
Age when interviewed: 94

I WAS born September 1, 1842, in Bastrop, Texas, on Colorado River. My pappy was named Harvey Wheeler and my mammy Carolina Sims. My brothers and sisters was named Alex, Taylor, Mary, Cicero, Tennessee, Sarah, Jeff, Ella, and Nora. My sister Liza was mulatto and Master Colonel Sims' son had three chillen by her. We never seen her no more after her last child was born. I found out, though, that she was in Canada.

I nursed three white chillen, Lulu, Helen Augusta, and Lola Sims. I done this before the War that set us free. We kids used to make extra money by toting gravel in our aprons. They'd give us dimes and silver nickles.

We lived in cedar log houses with dirt floors and double chimneys, and doors hung on wooden hinges. One side of our beds was bored in the walls and had one leg on the other. Them white folks give each nigger family a blanket in winter.

Our clothes was wool and cotton mixed. We had red rustic shoes, soles one-half inch thick. They'd go a-wick-a-wack. The mens had pants with one seam and a right-hand pocket. Boys wore shirts.

We ate hominy, mush, grits, and pone bread for the most part. Many of them ate out of one tray with wooden spoons. All victuals for field hands was fixed together.

Women broke in mules, throwed 'em down, and roped 'em. They'd do it better'n men. While Mammy made some hominy one day both my foots was scalded, and when they clipped them blisters, they just put some cotton round them and catched all dat yellow water and made me a yellow dress out of it. This was 'way back yonder in slavery, before the War.

Whenever white folks had a baby born, den all de old niggers had to come through the room and the master would be over behind the bed

111

and he'd say, "Here's a new little mistress or master you got to work for." You had to say, "Yessir, Master," and bow real low or the overseer would crack you. Them was slavery days, dog days.

My mammy belonged to Master Colonel Sam Sims and his old mean wife, Julia. My pappy belonged to Master Meke Smith and his good wife, Harriet. She was sure a good woman. I was named after her. Master Sam and Master Meke was partners. Every year them rich men would send so many wagons to New Mexico for different things. It took six months to go and come.

Slaves was punished by whip and starving. Decker was sure a mean slaveholder. He lived close to us. Master Sam didn't never whip me, but Miss Julia whipped me every day in the morning. During the War she beat us so terrible. She say, "Your master's out fighting and losing blood trying to save you from them Yankees, so you can get your'n here." Miss Julia would take me by my ears and but my head against the wall.

She wanted to whip my mother, but Old Master told her, "No sir." When his father done give my mammy to Master Sam, he told him not to beat her, and if he got to where he just had to, just bring her back and place her in his yard from where he got her.

White folks didn't allow you to read or write. Them what did know come from Virginny. Mistress Julia used to drill her chillen in spelling any words. At every word them chillen missed, she gived me a lick across the head for it. Meanest woman I ever seen in my whole life.

This skin I got now, it ain't my first skin. That was burnt off when I was a little child. Mistress used to have a fire made on the fireplace and she made me scour the brass round it and my skin just blistered. I just had to keep pulling it offen me.

We didn't had no church, though my pappy was a preacher. He preached in the quarters. Our baptizing song was "On Jordan's Stormy Bank I Stand" and "Hark from the Tomb." Now all dat was before the War. We had all our funerals at the graveyard. Everybody, chillen and all, picked up a clod of dirt and throwed in on top the coffin to help fill up the grave.

Talking about niggers running away, didn't my step-pappy run away? Didn't my uncle Gabe run away? The frost would just bite they toes most nigh off, too, whiles they was gone. They put Uncle Isom, my step-pappy, in jail and while's he was in there he killed a white guardsman. Then they put in the paper, "A nigger to kill," and our master seen it and bought him.

He was a double-strengthed man, he was so strong. He'd run off, so help you God. They had the bloodhounds after him once and he caught the hound what was leading and beat the rest of the dogs. The white folks run up on him before he knowed it and made them dogs eat his ear plumb out. But don't you know he got away anyhow.

One morning I was sweeping out the hall in the Big House and somebody come a-knocking on the front door and I goes to the door. There was Uncle Isom with rags all on his head. He said, "Tell Old Master here I am." I goes to Master's door and says, "Master Colonel Sam, Uncle Isom said here he am." He say, "Go round to the kitchen and tell black mammy to give you breakfast."

When he was through eating they give him three hundred lashes and, bless my soul, he run off again.

When we went to a party the nigger fiddlers would play a tune dat went like this:

> I fooled Old Master seven years,
> Fooled the overseer three;
> Hand me down my banjo,
> And I'll tickle your bel-lee.

We had the same doctors the white folks had and we wore asafetida and garlic and onions to keep from taking all them ailments.

I 'member the battle being fit. The white folks buried all the jewelry and silver and all the gold in the Blue Ridge Mountains, in Orange, Texas. Master made all us niggers come together and get ready to leave 'cause the Yankees was coming. We took a steamer. Now this was in slavery time, sure 'nough slavery. Then we got on a steamship and pulled out to Galveston. Then he told the captain to feed we niggers. We was on the bay, not the ocean. We left Galveston and went on trains for Houston.

After the War, Master Colonel Sims went to get the mail and so he call Daniel Ivory, the overseer, and say to him, "Go round to all the quarters and tell all the niggers to come up, I got a paper to read to 'em. They're free now, so you can get another job, 'cause I ain't got no more niggers which is my own." Niggers come up from the cabins nappy-headed, just like they gwine to the field. Master Colonel Sims say: "Caroline (that's my mammy), you is free as me. Pa said bring you back and I'se gwine do just that. So you go on and work and I'll pay you and your three oldest chillen ten dollars a month a head and four dollars for Harriet," that's me, and then he turned to the rest and say, "Now all you uns will receive ten dollars a head till the crop is laid by." Don't you know before he got halfway through, over half them niggers was gone.

Them Klu Klux Klans come and ask for water with the false stomachs and make like they was drinking three bucketsful. They done some terrible things, but God seen it all and marked it down.

We didn't had no law, we had "bureau." Why, in them days if somebody stole anything from you, they had to pay you and not the law. Now they done turned that round and you don't get nothing.

One day whiles Master was gone hunting, Mistress Julia told her brother to give Miss Harriett (me) a free whipping. She was a nigger killer. Master Colonel Sam come home and he said, "You infernal sons o' bitches, don't you know there is three hundred Yankees camped out here and if they knowed you'd whipped this nigger the way you done, they'd kill all us. If they find it out, I'll kill all you all." Old rich devils, I'm here but they is gone.

TOM ROBINSON

Interviewed near Hot Springs, Arkansas
Interviewed by Mary D. Hudgins
Age when interviewed: 88

IT'S MY understanding that I was born in Catawba County, North Carolina. As far as I remember, Newton was the nearest town. I was born on a place belonging to Jacob Sigmans. I can just barely remember my mother. I was not eleven when they sold me away from her. I can just barely remember her. But I do remember how she used to take us children and kneel down in front of the fireplace and pray. She'd pray that the time would come when everybody could worship the Lord under their own vine and fig tree — all of them free. It's come to me lots of times since. There she was a-praying, and on other plantations women was a-praying. All over the country the same prayer was being prayed. Guess the Lord done heard the prayer and answered it.

Old man Sigmans wasn't a bad master. Don't remember so much about him. I couldn't have been eleven when he sold me to Pinkney Setzer. He kept me for a little while and then he sold me to David Robinson. All three of them lived not so far apart in North Carolina. But pretty soon after he bought me old man Dave Robinson moved to Texas. We was there when the War started. We stayed there all during the War. I was set free there.

We lived in Cass County. It was pretty close to the Arkansas border, and 'twasn't far from Oklahoma. I remember well when they was first gathering them up for the War. We used to hear the cannon often. To be sure I was scared, right at first. Pretty soon we got used to it. Somebody even made up a song, "Listen to the Homemade Thunder." They'd sing it every time the cannon started roaring. There never was any fighting right around us. I never really saw any fighting.

Old man Dave Robinson was good to me. He didn't have a big farm — just owned me. Treated me almost like I was one of his own children. 'Course, I had to work. Sometimes he whipped me — but no more than he had to. I was just a child and any child has got to be made

115

to mind. He was good to me, and old Miss was good to me. All my masters was pretty good to me—lots better than the usual run. I kept the name Robinson, and I named my son Dave, so you might know which one I think the most of.

One day I was out milking the cows. Mr. Dave come down into the field, and he had a paper in his hands. "Listen to me, Tom," he said. "Listen to what I reads you." And he read from a paper all about how I was free. You can't tell how I felt. "You're jokin' me," I says. "No, I ain't," says he, "you're free." "No," says I, "it's a joke." "No," says he, "it's a law that I got to read this paper to you. Now listen while I read it again."

But still I wouldn't believe him. "Just go up to the house," says he, "and ask Mrs. Robinson. She'll tell you." So I went. "It's a joke," I says to her. "Did you ever know your master to tell you a lie?" she says. "No," says I, "I ain't." "Well," she says, "the War's over and you're free."

By that time I thought maybe she was telling me what was right. "Miss Robinson," says I, "can I go over to see the Smiths?"—they was a colored family that lived nearby. "Don't you understand," says she, "you're free. You don't have to ask me what you can do. Run along, child." And so I went. And do you know why I was a going? I wanted to find out if they was free too. I just couldn't take it all in. I couldn't believe we was all free alike.

Was I happy? Lord! You can take anything. No matter how good you treat it—it wants to be free. You can treat it good and feed it and give it everything it seems to want—but if you open the cage—it's happy.

After the War was over I farmed. I farmed all my life, till I got too old. I stopped three-four years ago. I didn't sharecrop, except just at first to get a start. I rented. I paid thirds and fourths. I always rented. I wasn't a sharecropper. Now I lives with my son—Dave Robinson—the one I named for my master. It was awful hard going after the War. But I got me a place—had to sharecrop for a year or two. But I worked hard and saved all I could. Pretty soon I had me enough that I could rent. I always raised the usual things—cotton and corn and potatoes and a little truck and that sort of thing—always raised enough to eat for us and the stock, and then some cotton for a cash crop.

My first wife, well, it was kind of funny. I wasn't more than nineteen. She had eleven children. Some of them was older than I was. But it wasn't too hard on me. They was all old enough to take care of themselves. I lived with that woman for seventeen years. Then she died.

I been married five times. Three of my children are living. One lives here in Hot Springs. Then there's one in Texarkana and there's one in Kansas City. Two of my children are dead. The youngest died just about last year. All my wives are dead.

ROBERT SHEPHERD

Interviewed at Athens, Georgia
Interviewed by Grace McCune
Age when interviewed: 91

MARSE JOE, he had three plantations, but he didn't live on none of 'em. He lived in Lexin'ton. He kept a overseer on each one of his plantations and dey had better be good to his niggers, or else Marse Joe would sure get 'em away from dere. He never allowed 'em to work us too hard, and in bad or real cold weather us didn't have to do no outside work 'cept everyday chores what had to be done, come rain or shine, like milkin', tendin' de stock, fetchin' in wood, and things like dat. He seed dat us had plenty of good somepin' to eat and all de clothes we needed. Us was lots better off in dem days dan us is now.

Old Marster, he had so many niggers dat he never knowed 'em all. One day he was a-ridin' along towards one of his plantations and he met one of his slaves, named William. Marse stopped him and asked him who he was. William said: "Why, Marster, I'se your nigger. Don't you know me?" Den Marster, he just laughed and said, "Well, hurry on home when you gets what you is gwine after." He was in a good humor dat way most all de time. I can see him a-ridin' dat little hoss of his'n what he called Button, and his little dog hoppin' along on three legs right side of de hoss. Dere weren't nothin' de matter with dat little dog; walkin' on three legs was just his way of gettin' round.

Marster never let none of de slave chillen on his plantation do no work, till dey got fifteen—dat was soon 'nough, he said. On all of his plantations dere was one old woman dat didn't have nothin' else to do but look after and cook for de nigger chillen whilst dey mammies was at work in de fields. Aunt Viney took care of us. She had a big old horn what she blowed when it was time for us to eat, and us knowed better dan to get so far off us couldn't hear dat horn, for Aunt Viney would sure tear us up. Marster had done told her she better fix us plenty to eat and give it to us on time.

Dere was a great long trough what went plum across de yard, and dat was where us et. For dinner us had peas or some other sort of vegetables, and corn bread. Aunt Viney crumbled up dat bread in de trough and poured de vegetables and pot likker over it. Den she blowed de horn and chillen come a-runnin' from every which way. If us et it all up, she had to put more victuals in de trough. At nights, she crumbled de corn bread in de trough and poured buttermilk over it. Us never had nothin' but corn bread and buttermilk at night. Sometimes dat trough would be a sight, 'cause us never stopped to wash our hands, and before us had been eatin' more dan a minute or two what was in de trough would look like real mud what had come off our hands. Sometimes Aunt Viney would fuss at us and make us clean it out.

Dere was a big sandbar down on de crick what made a fine place to play, and wadin' in de branches was lots of fun. Us frolicked up and down dem woods and had all sorts of good times—anything to keep away from Aunt Viney 'cause she was sure to have us fetchin' in wood or sweepin' de yards if us was handy where she could find us. If us was out of her sight she never bothered about dem yards and things.

Us was scared to answer dat horn when us got in Marster's tobacco. He raised lots of tobacco and rationed it out to mens, but he never 'lowed chillen to have none till dey was big enough to work in de fields. Us found out how to get in his tobacco house and us kept on gettin' his tobacco before it was dried out till he missed it. Den he told Aunt Viney to blow dat horn and call up all de chillen. "I'se gwine to whip every one of 'em," he would declare. After us got dere and he seed dat green tobacco had done made us so sick us couldn't eat, he just couldn't beat us. He just laughed and said, "It's good enough for you."

Aunt Martha, she done de milkin' and helped Aunt Nancy cook for de slaves. Dey had a big long kitchen up at de Big House where de overseer lived. De slaves what worked in de field never had to do dere own cookin'. It was all done for 'em in dat big kitchen. Dey cooked some of de victuals in big old washpots and dere was sure a plenty for all. All de cookin was done in big fireplaces what had racks made inside to hang pots on and dey had big old ovens for bakin' and thick iron skillets, and long-handled fryin' pans. You just can't imagine how good things was cooked dat way on de open fire. Nobody never had no better hams and other meat dan our marster kept in dem big old smokehouses, and his slaves had meat just like white folks did. Dem cooks knowed dey had to cook a plenty and have it ready when it was time for de slaves to come in from de fields. Miss Ellen, she was de overseer's wife, went out in de kitchen and looked over everything to see that it was all right and den she blowed de bugle. When de slaves heared dat bugle, dey come in a-singin' from de fields. Dey was happy 'cause dey knowed Miss Ellen had a good dinner ready for 'em.

De slave quarters was long rows of log cabins with chimblies made out of sticks and red mud. Dem chimblies was all de time catchin' fire. Dey didn't have no glass windows. For a window dey just cut a openin' in a log and fixed a piece of plank across it so it would slide when dey wanted to open or close it. Doors was made out of rough planks, beds was rough homemade frames nailed to de side of de cabins, and mattresses was coarse, home-wove ticks filled with wheat straw. Dey had good homemade cover. Dem beds slept mighty good.

Dere weren't many folks sick dem days, especially amongst de slaves. When one did die, folks would go twelve or fifteen miles to de buryin'. Marster would say: "Take de mules and wagons and go; but mind you, take good care of dem mules." He never seemed to care if us went— fact was, he said us ought to go. If a slave died on our place, nobody went to de fields till after de buryin'. Marster never let nobody be buried till dey had been dead twenty-four hours, and if dey had people from some other place, he waited till dey could get dere. He said it weren't right to hurry 'em off into de ground too quick after dey died. Dere warn't no undertakers dem days. De homefolks just laid de corpse out on de coolin' board till de coffin was made. A coolin' board was made out of a long straight plank raised a little at de head and had legs fixed to make it set straight. Dey wrapped woman corpses in windin' sheets. Uncle Squire, de man what done all de wagon work and buildin' on our place, made coffins. Dey was just plain wood boxes dat dey painted to make 'em look nice.

White preachers conducted the funerals, and most of de time our own marster done it, 'cause he was a preacher hisself. When de funeral was done preached, dey sung "Harps from de Tomb." Den dey put de coffin in a wagon and drive slow and careful to de graveyard. De preacher prayed at de grave and de mourners sung, "I'se Born to Die and Lay Dis Body Down." Dey never had no outside box for de coffin to be set in, but dey put planks on top of de coffin before dey started shovelin' in de dirt.

Fourth Sundays was our meetin' days, and everybody went to church. Us went to our white folks' church and rode in a wagon behind dere carriage. Dere was two Baptist preachers—one of 'em was Mr. John Gibson and de other was Mr. Patrick Butler. Marse Joe was a Methodist preacher hisself, but dey all went to de same church together. De niggers set in de gallery. When dey had done give de white folks de sacrament, dey called de niggers down from de gallery and give dem de sacrament, too. Church days was sure 'nough big meetin' days 'cause everybody went. Dey preached three times a day: at eleven in de mornin', three in de evenin', and den again at night. De biggest meetin' house crowds was when dey had baptizin', and dat was right often. Dey dammed up de crick on Saturday so as it would be deep enough on Sunday and dey done de baptizin' before dey preached de three o'clock sermon. At dem baptizins dere was all sorts of shoutin', and dey would sing "Roll Jordan, Roll," "De Livin' Waters," and "Lord I'se Comin' Home."

When de crops was laid by and most of de hardest work of de year done up, den was camp-meetin' time, 'long in de last of July and sometimes in August. Dat was when us had de biggest times of all. Dey had great big long tables and just everything good to eat. Dey would kill five or six hogs and have 'em carried dere to be barbecued, and Marster carried his own cooks along. After de white folks et dey fed de niggers, and dere was always a plenty for all. Marster sure looked after all his niggers good at dem times.

When de camp-meetin' was over, den come de big baptizin': white folks first, den niggers. One time dere was a old slave woman what got so scared when dey got out in de crick dat somebody had to pull her foots out under her to get her under de water. She got out from dere and testified dat it was de devil a-holdin' her back.

De white ladies had nice silk dresses to wear to church. Slave womans had new calico dresses what dey wore with hoopskirts dey made out of grapevines. Dey wore poke bonnets with ruffles on 'em and if de weather was sort of cool, dey wore shawls. Marster always wore his linen duster. Dat was his white coat, made cutaway style with long tails. De cloth for most all of de clothes was made at home. Marse Joe raised lots of sheep and de wool was used to make cloth for de winter clothes. Us had a great long loom house where some of de slaves didn't do nothin' but weave cloth. Some carded bats, some done de spinnin', and dere was more of 'em to do de sewin'.

Miss Ellen, she looked after all dat, and she cut out most of de clothes. She seed dat us had plenty to wear. Sometimes Marster would go to de sewin' house, and Mist'ess would tell him to get on away from dere and look after his own work, dat her and Aunt Julia could run dat loom house. Marster he just laughed den and told us chillen what was hangin' around de door to just listen to dem womans cackle.

Us had water buckets, called piggens, what was made out of cedar and had handles on de sides. Sometimes us sawed off little vinegar kegs and put handles on 'em. Us loved to drink out of gourds. Dere was lots of gourds raised every year. Some of 'em was so big dey was used to keep eggs in and for lots of things us uses baskets for now. Dem little gourds made fine dippers.

Dem corn shuckin's was sure 'nough big times. When us got all de corn gathered up and put in great long piles, den de gettin' ready started. Why, dem womans cooked for days, and de mens would get de shoats ready to barbecue. Marster would send us out to get de slaves from de farms round about dere. De place was all lit up with light-wood knot torches and bonfires, and dere was 'citement a-plenty when all niggers get to singin' and shoutin' as dey made de shucks fly.

One of dem songs went somethin' like dis: "Oh! my head, my poor head. Oh! my poor head is affected." Dere weren't nothin' wrong with our heads—dat was just our way of lettin' our overseer know us wanted some liquor. Purty soon he would come 'round with a big horn of whiskey, and dat made de poor head well, but it weren't long before it got worse again, and den us got another horn of whiskey. When de corn was all shucked, den us et all us could and, let me tell you, dat was some good eatin's. Den us danced de rest of de night.

Next day when us all felt so tired and bad, Marster, he would tell us about stayin' up all night, but Mist'ess took up for us, and dat tickled Old Marster. He just laughed and said: "Will you listen to dat woman?" Den he would make some of us sing one of dem songs us had done been singin' to dance by. It goes sort of like dis: "Turn your pardner round! Steal round de corner, 'cause dem Johnson gals is hard to beat! Just glance round and have a good time! Dem gals is hard to find!"

Us had big possum hunts, and us sure catched a heap of 'em. De gals cooked 'em with 'taters and dey just made your mouth water. I sure wish I had one now. Rabbits was good, too. Marster didn't allow no huntin' with guns, so us just took dogs when us went huntin'. Rabbits was kilt with sticks and rocks 'cept when big snow come. Dey was easy to track to dey beds den, and us could just reach in and pull 'em out. When us catch 'nough of 'em, us had big rabbit suppers.

I didn't have no sure 'nough weddin'. Me and Julie just jumped over de broom in front of Marster and us was married. Dat was all dere was to it. Dat was de way most of de slave folks got married dem days. Us knowed better dan to ask de gal when us wanted to get married. Us just told our Marster and he done de askin'. Den, if it was all right with de gal, Marster called all de other niggers up to de Big House to see us jump over de broom.

If a slave wanted to get married to somebody on another place, den he told Marster and his marster would talk to de gal's marster. Whatever dey agreed on was all right. If neither one of 'em would sell one of de slaves what wanted to get married, den dey let 'em go ahead and jump over de broom, and de man just visited his wife on her marster's place, mostly on Wednesday and Saturday nights. If it was a long piece off, he didn't get dere so often. Dey had to have passes den, 'cause de patterollers would get 'em sure if dey didn't. Dat meant a thrashin' and dey didn't miss layin' on de sticks when dey catch a nigger.

De big war was about over when dem Yankees come by our place and just went through everything. Dey called all de slaves together and told 'em dey was free and didn't belong to nobody no more. And said de slaves could take all dey wanted from de smokehouses and barns and de Big House, and could go when and where dey wanted to go. Dey tried to hand us out all de meat and hams, but us told 'em us weren't hungry, 'cause Marster had always done give us all us wanted. When dey couldn't make none of us take nothin', dey said it was de strangest thing dey had done ever seed and dat dat man Echols must have sure been good to his niggers.

When dem Yankees had done gone off Marster come out to our place. He blowed de bugle to call us all up to de house. He couldn't hardly talk, 'cause somebody had done told him dat dem Yankees couldn't talk his niggers into stealin' nothin'. Marster said he never knowed before how good us loved him. He told us he had done tried to be good to us and had done de best he could for us and dat he was mighty proud of de way every one of us had done behaved ourselfs. He said dat de War was over now and us was free and could go anywhere us wanted to, but dat us didn't have to go if us wanted to stay dere. He said he would pay us for our work and take care of us if us stayed or, if us wanted to work on shares, he would allow us to work some land dat way. A few of dem niggers drifted off, but most of 'em stayed right dere till dey died.

Me, I stayed right dere till after Marster died. He was sick a long, long time and one morning Old Mist'ess, she called to me. "Robert," she said, "you ain't gwine to have no Marster long, 'cause he's about gone." I called all de niggers up to de Big House and when dey was all in de yard, Mist'ess, she said: "Robert, you been with us so long, you can come in and see him before he's gone for good." When I got in dat room I knowed de Lord had done laid His hand on my good old marster, and he was a-goin' to dat home he used to preach to us niggers about, and it appeared to me like my heart would just bust. When de last breath was done gone, I went back out in de yard and told de other niggers, and dere was sure cryin' and prayin' amongst 'em, 'cause all of 'em loved Marster. Dat was sure one big funeral. Mist'ess said she wanted all of Marster's old slaves to go, 'cause he loved 'em so, and all of us went. Some what had done been gone years come back for Marster's funeral.

Next day, after de funeral was over, Mist'ess, she said: "Robert, I want you to stay on with me 'cause you know how he wanted his work done." Den Mist'ess daughter and her husband Mr. Dickenson, come dere to stay. None of de niggers liked dat Mr. Dickenson so most of 'em left and den, about two years after Marster died, Mist'ess went to Atlanta to stay with another of her daughters, and she died dere. When Mist'ess left, I left too and come on here to Athens, and I been here ever since.

BILL SIMMS

Interviewed in Ottawa, Kansas
Interviewed by Leta Gray
Age when interviewed: 97

MY NAME is Bill Simms. I was born in Osceola, Missouri, March 16, 1839. I lived on the farm with my mother and my master, whose name was Simms. I had an older sister, about two years older than I was. My master needed some money so he sold her, and I have never seen her since except just a time or two.

On the plantation we raised cows, sheep, cotton, tobacco, corn, which were our principal crops. There was plenty of wild hogs, turkey, and deer, and other game. The deer used to come up and feed with the cattle in the feed yards, and we could get all the wild hogs we wanted by simply shooting them in the timber.

A man who owned ten slaves was considered wealthy, and if he got hard up for money, he would advertise and sell some slaves, like my oldest was sold on the block with her children. She sold for eleven hundred dollars, a baby in her arms sold for three hundred dollars. Another sold for six hundred dollars and the other for a little less than that. My master was offered fifteen hundred dollars for me several times, but he refused to sell me, because I was considered a good, husky slave. My family is all dead, and I am the only one living.

The slaves usually lived in a two-room house made of native lumber. The houses were all small. A four- or five-room house was considered a mansion. We made our own clothes, had spinning wheels and raised and combed our own cotton, clipped the wool from our sheeps' backs, combed and spun it into cotton and wool clothes. We never knew what boughten clothes were. I learned to make shoes when I was just a boy and I made the shoes for the whole family. I used to chop wood and make rails and do all kinds of farm work.

I had a good master. Most of the masters were good to their slaves. When a slave got too old to work they would give him a small cabin in the plantation and have the other slaves to wait on him. They would furnish him with victuals and clothes until he died.

Slaves were never allowed to talk to white people other than their masters or someone their masters knew, as they were afraid the white man might have the slave run away. The masters aimed to keep their slaves in ignorance and the ignorant slaves were all in favor of the Rebel army. Only the more intelligent were in favor of the Union army.

When the War started, my master sent me to work for the Confederate army. I worked most of the time for three years off and on, hauling cannons, driving mules, hauling ammunition and provisions. The Union army pressed in on us and the Rebel army moved back. I was sent home. When the Union army came close enough I ran away from home and joined the Union army. There I drove a six-mule team and worked at wagon work, driving ammunition and all kinds of provisions until the war ended.

Then I returned home to my old master, who had stayed there with my mother. My master owned about four hundred acres of good land, and had had ten slaves. Most of the slaves stayed at home. My master hired me to work for him. He gave my mother forty acres of land with a cabin on it and sold me forty acres, for twenty dollars, when I could pay him. This was timbered land and had lots of good trees for lumber, especially walnut. One tree on this ground was worth one hundred dollars. If I could only get it cut and marketed, I could pay for my land.

My master's wife had been dead for several years and they had no children, the nearest relative being a nephew. They wanted my master's land and was afraid he would give it all away to us slaves, so they killed him, and would have killed us if we had stayed at home. I took my mother and ran into the adjoining Claire County. We settled there and stayed for some time, but I wanted to see Kansas, the state I had heard so much about.

I couldn't get nobody to go with me, so I started out afoot across the prairies for Kansas. After I got some distance from home it was all prairie. I had to walk all day long following buffalo trail. At night I would go off a little ways from the trail and lay down and sleep. In the morning I'd wake up and could see nothing but the sun and prairie. Not a house, not a tree, no living thing, not even could I hear a bird.

I had little to eat. I had a little bread in my pocket. I didn't even have a pocket knife, no weapon of any kind. I was not afraid, but I wouldn't start out that way again. The only shade I could find in the daytime was the rosinweed on the prairie. I would lay down so it would throw the shade in my face and rest, then get up and go again.

It was in the spring of the year in June. I came to Lawrence, Kansas, where I stayed two years working on the farm. In 1874 I went to work for a man by the month at thirty-five dollars a month and I made more money than the owner did, because the grasshoppers ate up the crops. I was hired to cut up the corn for him, but the grasshoppers ate it up first. He could not pay me for some time. Grasshoppers were so thick you couldn't step on the ground without stepping on about a dozen at each step. I got my money and come to Ottawa in December 1874, about Christmas time.

My master's name was Simms and I was known as Simms' Bill, just like horses. When I came out here I just changed my name from Simms' Bill, to Bill Simms. Ottawa was very small at the time I came here, and there were several Indians close by that used to come to town.

The Indians held their war dance on what is now the courthouse grounds. I planted the trees that are now standing on the courthouse grounds. There were few farms fenced and what were, were on the streams. The prairie land was all open. Ottawa didn't have many business houses. There was also an oil mill where they brought castor beans and made castor oil. There was one hotel, which was called Leafton House.

The people lived pretty primitive. We didn't have kerosene. Our only lights were tallow candles, mostly grease lamps. They were just a pan with grease in it, and one end of the rag dragging out over the side which we would light. There were no sewers at that time. I had no chance to go to school when a boy, but after I came to Kansas I was too old to go to school, and I had to work, but I attended night school, and learned to read and write and figure.

The farm land was nearly all broke up by ox teams, using about six oxen on a plow. In Missouri we lived near the Santa Fe Trail, and the settlers traveling on the trail used oxen, and some of them used cows. The cows seem to stand the road better than the oxen and also gave some milk. The travelers usually aimed to reach the prairie states in the spring, so they could have grass for their oxen and horses during the summer.

I have lived here since I came here. I was married when I was about thirty years old. I married a slave girl from Georgia. Back in Missouri, if a slave wanted to marry a woman on another plantation, he had to ask the master, and if both masters agreed they were married. The man stayed at his owner's, and the wife at her owner's. He could go to see her on Saturday night and Sunday. Sometimes only every two weeks.

If a man was a big strong man, neighboring plantation owners would ask him to come over and see his gals, hoping that he might want to marry one of them, but if a Negro was a small man he was not cared for as a husband, as they valued their slaves as only for what they could do, just like they would horses. When they were married and if they had children they belonged to the man who owned the woman.

Osceola is where the saying originated, "I'm from Missouri, show me." After the War the smart guys came through and talked the people into voting bonds, but there was no railroad built. Most counties paid their bonds, but the county in which Osceola stands refused to pay for their bonds because there was no railroad built, and they told the collectors to "show me the railroad and we will pay," and that is where "show me" originated.

My wife died when we had three children. She had had to work hard all her life and she said she didn't want her children to have to work as hard as she had, and I promised her on her deathbed, that I would educate our girls. So I worked and sent the girls to school.

My two girls both graduated from Ottawa University, the oldest one being the first colored girl to ever graduate from that school. After graduation she went to teach school in Oklahoma, but only got twenty-five dollars a month, and I had to work and send her money to pay her expenses. The younger girl also graduated and went to teach school, but she did not teach school long, until she married a well-to-do farmer in Oklahoma. The older girl got her wages raised until she got one hundred and twenty-five dollars per month.

I have worked at farm work and tree husbandry all my life. I have been living alone about twenty-five years. I don't know how old I was, but my oldest daughter had written my mother before she died, and got our family record, which my mother kept in her old Bible. Each year she writes me and tells me on my birthday how old I am.

BEN SIMPSON

Interviewed at Madisonville, Texas
Interviewer not identified
Age when interviewed: 90

BOSS, I'SE born in Georgia, in Norcross, and I'se ninety years old. My father's name was Roger Stielszen and my mother's name was Betty. Master Earl Stielszen captures them in Africa and brung them to Georgia. He got killed and my sister and me went to his son. His son was a killer. He got in trouble there in Georgia and got him two good-stepping horses and the covered wagon. Then he chains all he slaves around the necks and fastens the chains to the horses and makes them walk all the way to Texas. My mother and my sister had to walk. Emma was my sister. Somewhere on the road it went to snowing and Master wouldn't let us wrap anything around our feet. We had to sleep on the ground, too, in all that snow.

Master have a great, long whip platted out of rawhide, and when one of the niggers fall behind or give out, he hit him with that whip. It take the hide every time he hit a nigger. Mother, she give out on the way, about the line of Texas. Her feet got raw and bleeding and her legs swole plumb out of shape. Then Master he just take out he gun and shot her, and whilst she lay dying he kicks her two, three times and say, "Damn a nigger what can't stand nothing." Boss, you know that man, he wouldn't bury Mother, just leave her laying where he shot her at. You know, then there wasn't no law against killing nigger slaves.

He come plumb to Austin through that snow. He taken up farming and changes he name to Alex Simpson, and changes our names, too. He cut logs and built he home on the side of them mountains. We never had no quarters. When nighttime come he locks the chain 'round our necks and then locks it 'round a tree. Boss, our bed were the ground. All he feed us was raw meat and green corn. Boss, I ate many a green weed. I was hungry. He never let us eat at noon; he worked us all day without stopping. We went naked, that the way he worked us. We never had any clothes.

He brands us. He brand my mother before us left Georgia. Boss, that nearly killed her. He brand her in the breast, then between the shoulders. He brand all us.

My sister, Emma, was the only woman he have 'till he marries. Emma was wife of all seven Negro slaves. He sold her when she's about fifteen, just before her baby was born. I never seen her since.

Boss, Master was an outlaw. He come to Texas and deal in stolen horses. Just before he's hung for stealing horses, he marries a young Spanish gal. He sure mean to her, whips her 'cause she want him to leave he slaves alone and live right. Bless her heart, she's the best gal in the world. She cry and cry every time Master go off. She let us loose and she feed us good one time while he's gone. Missy Selena, she turn us loose and we wash in the creek close by. She just fasten the chain on us and give us great big pot of cooked meat and corn, and up he rides. Never says a word but come to see what us eating. He pick up he whip and whip her till she falls. If I could have got loose I'd killed him. I swore if I ever got loose I'd kill him. But before long after that he fails to come home, and some people finds him hanging to a tree. Boss, that long after war time he got hung. He didn't let us free. We wore chains all the time. When we work, we drug them chains with us. At night he lock us to a tree to keep us from running off. He didn't have to do that. We were afraid to run. We knew he'd kill us. Besides, he brands us, and they no way to get it off. It's put there with a hot iron. You can't get it off.

If a slave die, Master made the rest of us tie a rope 'round he feet and drug him off. Never buried one; it was too much trouble.

Master always say he be rich after the war. He stealing all the time. He have a whole mountainside where he keep he stock. Missy Selena tell us one day we supposed to be free, but he didn't turn us loose.

I had a hard time then. All I had to eat was what I could find and steal. I was afraid of everybody. I just went wild and to the woods, but, thank God, a bunch of men take they dogs and run me down. They carry me to they place. General Houston had some niggers and he made them feed me. He made them keep me till I get well and able to work. Then he give me a job. I marry one of the gals before I leaves them. I'm plumb out of place there at my own wedding. Yes, sir, boss, it wasn't one year before that I'm the wild nigger. We had thirteen children.

I farm all my life after that. I didn't know nothing else to do. I made plenty cotton, but now I'm too old. Me and my wife is alone now. This old nigger gets the little pension from the government. I not got much longer to stay here. I'se ready to see God, but I only hope my old master ain't there to torment me again.

GUS SMITH

Interviewed at Rolla, Missouri
Interviewer not identified
Age when interviewed: 92

I WAS born in 1845, on de Fourth of July, near Rich Fountain, Osage County, Missouri, not far from Jefferson City. My father's name was Jim Messersmith, and my mother's maiden name was Martha Williams. I was called August Messersmith until I was old enough to vote, den I changed it to plain Gus Smith. My friends nicknamed me "Chinie" and I am called dat today.

My master's name was Bill Messersmith and he called hisself a Pennsylvania Dutchman. His father settled in Missouri, near Jefferson City, many years before de War. He owned 1,500 acres of land. The old man, my master's father, had a good many slaves but de chillen didn't have so many after de old man died. Rufus, the old man's son and my master's brother, took one of de Negro boys; his sister, Manisee, took a Negro girl. These two, Rufus and Manisee, never married and lived with my master. Zennie, another sister, took a girl and a boy. She married a man by de name of Goodman and my master took my father and my mother.

My master's father, before he died, told his chillen dat at his death he wanted each child to put their slaves out to work until dey earned eight hundred dollars apiece, to earn their own freedom; in dat way each slave paid it demselves. He did not believe it was right to keep dem in slavery all their lives. But de War came and dey were free without having to work it out.

We all wore homespun clothes, made of wool mostly. Mother carded, spun, and wove all our clothes. My master let us come and go pretty much as we pleased. In fact we had much more freedom dan de most of de slaves had in those days. He let us go to other places to work when we had nothing to do at home and we kept our money we earned, and spent it to suit ourselves. We had it so much better dan other slaves dat our neighbors would not let their slaves associate with

129

us, for fear we would put devilment in their heads, for we had too much freedom. My father and mother had their own cabin to live in with their family, but de rest of de slaves stayed with our mistress. My father's relations lived within ten miles of us. Dey come to see us but dat was about all de company we had.

We used to sing all the old plantation songs, but my father and mother were not such good singers. We all had good times along with de work. During Christmas time and de whole month of January, it was de rulin' to give de slaves a holiday in our part of de country. A whole month, to go and come as much as we pleased and go for miles as far as we wanted to, but we had better be back by de first of February. If we wanted to go through a territory where it was hard to travel, or get by, we got a pass from our master.

We had quiltin's, dancin', makin' rails, for days at a time. We don't have nothin' to eat now like we did then. All kinds of game, wild ducks, geese, squirrels, rabbits, possum, pigeons, and fried chicken. My, women in those days could cook. Great big pound cakes a foot and a half high. You don't see such things, nowadays.

I remember my father shooting so many pigeons at once that my mother just fed dem to the hogs. Just shoot the game from our back yard. I have seen de wild pigeons so thick dey looked like storm clouds coming. I've seen dem so thick dey broke tree limbs down. Ducks and geese de same way. We could kill dem by tow sacks full, with clubs. White folks and colored folks came to these gatherings, from miles around, sat up all night dancin', and drinkin'. People kept whiskey by de barrel in those days. You see in those days dey just loaded up ten or twelve bushel of corn, took it to de "still-house" and traded it for a barrel of whiskey. Not much selling in those days, everything was traded, even to labor. Our folks would tell us to go and help so and so and we done it.

Mother was de cook in those days at our place. De hewed log house we lived in was very big, about five or six rooms. In times of our holidays, we always had our own musicians. Sometimes we sent ten or twelve miles for a fiddler. He'd stay a week or so in one place and den he would go on to de next farm, maybe four or five miles away, and dey had a good time for a week. When we didn't have much work, we would get up about five o'clock every morning, but in busy season we had to be up and ready to work at daybreak. There was plenty of work for every one den, even to de little darkies, if only to pull weeds. We raised wheat, corn, cotton, tobacco, cabbage, potatoes, sheep, hogs, and cattle. Had plenty of everything to eat.

Our closest neighbors was de Thorntons. Old man Thornton did not allow his slaves to go no place. He was a rough man, a low heavy-set fellow, weighed about one hundred and sixty pounds. He was mean to his slaves. He whipped dem all de time. I've seen their clothes sticking to their backs, from blood and scabs, being cut up with de cowhide. He just whipped dem because he could. Us used to say he always give his niggers a "breakfast spell ever' mornin'!" Dat is he whipped dem every morning. I remember he had a nigger woman about seventy years old on his place. De Thorntons did not feed their slaves; dey was nearly starved. One night that old woman was so hungry she stole a chicken from her master, Old Thornton, and was cooking it in her cabin. He found it out some way and started to her cabin and caught her, while she had it on boiling. He was so mad, he told her to get a spoon and eat every bite before she stopped. It was scalding hot but he made her do it. She died right away; her insides was burned.

Why, Old Thornton was dat mean dat he killed his own son. He just beat him to death with de whip stock of dat cowhide, a whip made of buckskin. It was like dis. De boy had a girl he was courtin' in another town. He started to see her on Saturday noon. His daddy told him to be back by Sunday night. But de boy did not get back before Monday mornin', ten o'clock. His father was in de field working and saw him coming down de road. He went to meet him and met him at de gate. He asked why he did not get back sooner and lit into beating him with the whip stock, de part dat would be de whip handle. He beat him so hard dat de boy died after ten hours. It aroused de neighborhood and dey began to plan a lynching party. He got wind of it some way and got all his slaves together and pulled out. He left dat place and no one ever knowed where he went. Dat happened before de end of de War.

There was a lot of runaway slaves in those days. I never see any of dem but I heard de folks talk about dem. Many passed through our part of de country. In time of slavery, people were sold like cattle or hogs. There was no sale bills dat we seen, because folks in dem days was usually honest and did not have a lot of red tape in buying and selling. Our master would not sell any of us. He did not believe in separating us, and tried to keep us together. He didn't have any trouble with his slaves at all. He was as good a man as ever lived and we did pretty much as we pleased.

He married before de War, but his first wife died a few months later. He married a year after his wife died. He went to Pennsylvania and came back and went to California for about a year. Before he left he made my father boss. My father stayed on de place and took care of everything. He was boss all during de War.

When the battle of Wilson Creek was fought up near Springfield, most all soldiers passed by our house. After dey passed den came de bushwhackers. Dey stole all de niggers dey could, running dem down

South to sell. Dey came to our place in de morning; it must have been about 1862–63. De whole family of colored folks was home, 'cepting my father. Dey looked across de road and seen another house and asked us whose house it was. We told dem it was our master's house. Dey saw we had a mare in de yard and told us to saddle her up. And dey told my oldest brother to be ready to go with dem when dey come back. Dey went halfway to my master's house and for some reason wheeled and came back. My mother looked out de door and seen them coming and said: "Here they come."

She said to my oldest brother, "Get under dat puncheon floor, maybe dey won't take August," meaning me. I was about twelve or thirteen years old den. We had a great big hearth, de rocks and puncheon came right up to it. My mother raised de one end of a puncheon and my brother hid there under de floor. De bushwhackers came back to de house and searched everywhere, failed to find him, even raised de floor and looked under, but my brother had crawled so far up in de corner dey did not see him. Dey asked my mother where he was and said, "By God! We want to know." Mother answered and said she sent him down to de field to get some corn for de hogs and told me to run down there and look for him.

Well I did. I run down in dat field and am going yet. I stayed out in dat woods for four days and nights with nothing to eat but what wild grapes and hazel nuts I could find. I knew better dan to go back dere, but I did not know where to go. I fell on a plan to go to my young missus, Zennie. Dey lived off de main road, two miles from where we lived. When I got to her home, it was in de evening about four o'clock. I saw my cousin, Melie, fifteen or sixteen years old, but was afraid to speak to her. I saw her out a piece from de barn, but I wouldn't let her see me. I stayed all night in de barn, and next morning I peeped out de window and saw her again. She was picking beans. I hollered and she recognized me and asked me if I wasn't August. I said yes. She told me to come on out and go with her, dat my mother and all of dem was at dere house den. My oldest brother, Jim, was dere too. He was four years older dan me.

Den I went down to de house and dey soon fixed me something to eat. But only a little because dey were afraid it might make me sick. My mother told me to stay with Miss Zennie. Miss Zennie had married de second time to a man by de name of George McGee. Her first husband, Dave Goodman, was killed right at de start of de War by a gang of robbers something like de bushwhackers, who went in gangs of ten and fifteen, stealing niggers or anything else dey could get their hands on.

George McGee and my brother Jim hid out in de bluffs at Rollin's Ferry, a place where ferryboats ran. George McGee hid because he did not want to go in de army. So he takes my brother and hides in de bluffs. Dey both came to de house for provisions about twelve o'clock dat night and took me with dem. We camped out dat night and next morning dey said to me: "You stay here. Dey is out of meat at de house." So dey went back to de house and killed and dressed a young heifer and came back at night to get me. We had a good time eating supper and playing.

Along in de night I heard something like horses hoofs hitting de ground. I told my mother and she said, "You don't hear nothing." George McGee, de young marster said, "Wait, he is right. I hears something too!" We jumped up and went out and down a steep hollow and made it back to our camp dat night yet. Next morning we wondered who it could have been dat we heard. Dat night we went back to see how de folks was getting on and found out it was my own father and our own marster who had come a-hunting for us. If we had known, we would not have run.

My master told his sister, Miss Zennie, to keep us hid out of de way, that we were doing all right. I stayed in dat bluff about two years, until de close of de War. I never saw my father and master for over a year. I saw my mother every time I went to de house for something to eat, about twelve o'clock at night. My father had to hide out too. He kept de stock out in de bushes, watching after de master's affairs while he was away.

We stayed hid until dey took General Lee. Den we went back to Old Master's house and it was not long until peace was declared. Our house was about a quarter of a mile from de master's, on a farm he had bought from an old Dutchman, about one hundred and sixty acres. One morning, Old Master come over early and said, "Jim, by God! You are a free man dis morning, as free as I am. I can't hold you any longer. Now take your family and go over on dat hundred and sixty acres I bought and go to work." He was giving us all a chance to pay out de farm for ourselves a home. My father said, "There's nothing to go with it to help clear it and live." To which Old Master answered: "There's de smokehouse, take all you want and I'll furnish you with everything else you need for a year, until you get a start." He allowed us to use anything to work with he had on his place.

Den we went to work. Old Master said, "I've got all de land my heart could wish but none of it is cleared off. Go down dere with your boys and I'll send two men, both white (Irishmen, Jim and Tom Norman) and all of you clear off dat land. I'll give you five years' lease to clear all you can. All you clear, you can have half." Well, we cleared fifty acres dat winter. We made rails, fenced it, and put it all in corn dat first year. There was six of us to do dis; my cousin joined my father, brother, and myself, and de two white men.

We had it cleared by the first of March—all ready to plow in 1865. My father raised his own sheep and cotton, and from dis my mother made our clothes. Father cleared thirty acres on his place de same year and sowed it all in wheat. De first year we got 817 bushels of wheat and 1,500 bushel of corn, it was all new land. Corn really growed in dem days. We hoed it by hand. You don't see corn like dat now. We worked out every little weed. Every little darky worked in dem days.

My grandad, Godfry, owned a place called de old Potter's place, near Vichey Springs, Vichey, Missouri, not far from where we lived. He bought it from a man who used to make pottery. Grandfather made his own mill to grind grain for bread. In dose days there was no steam operated mills and few water mills. Sometimes we had to go as much as twenty miles to grind corn. So grandfather made his own burr to grind corn and wheat. It was as big as any burr in de large mills, but it was turned by hand power. It was made of limestone rock, a great big stone about two and a half foot across. De top burr would probably weigh about three or four hundred pounds. De bottom case would weigh a thousand pounds or more. There was a hole in de top stone, where de grain flowed freely to de bottom and ground out on the big thick stone below. I ground many a bushel of meal on it myself. I don't know how Grandfather got de large stones in place, for it was there as long as I could remember. I just wonder if it isn't some place there yet. I would like to go and find out and see de old burr again.

Those were hard days, when folks had to go on foot twenty miles to mill. I remember in my early days, we used cattle for teams to haul, start at four o'clock in de morning, drive all day, stay overnight and grind de next day. Sometimes de crowd ahead of us was so big we had to stay over for three or four days. Sometimes we would be until eleven or twelve at night getting home. Gone at least two days and one night. I had to make trips like dis many times.

Sometimes we could take a couple of bushel of corn and go horseback, but twice a year, spring and fall, we would take eight or ten bushel of wheat, and six or eight bushel of corn or, according to what we needed, and take de cattle and a old wooden axle wagon, walking and driving de cattle all de way dere and back. We drove or led dem with only a rope around dem.

De last trip I made millin', I drove for Bill Fannins, a yoke of young three-year-old cattle. Wasn't even broke. Went twenty-five miles, drove all de way, walking, while he sat up in de wagon. Sometimes de wagon dragged in de mud—de old wooden axle burying so deep we couldn't hardly get it out—going through timber and dodging brush. Some folks went even further dan dat. Sometimes a mill might be four or five miles from you but dey got out of fix and you would have to go to another one. Maybe twenty-five miles or more.

There was not many good doctors in those days, but my grandfather was an old-fashioned herb doctor. I remember him well. I was about twenty-five years old when he died. Everybody knew him in dat country and he doctored among white people, one of de best doctors of his kind. He went over thirty miles around to people who sent for him. He was seldom at home. Lots of cases dat other doctors gave up, he went and raised them. He could cure anything.

When I was sick one time, I was den about eighteen or nineteen years old, my folks had Dr. Boles, from Lane's Prairie and Dr. Mayweather from Vichey, to come and tend me. Dey both gave me up. I had typhoid and pneumonia. Dese doctors were de best to be found but dey could do nothing and I was as good as dead. My grandfather was gone, had come to Rolla, doctoring Charley Stroback's child whose clothes had caught fire and he was burned badly. Grandfather could "blow out" fire.

He got home about four o'clock in de morning after de doctors had done give me up. He felt my pulse and said he didn't know whether I was dead or alive. No pulse, but he said I felt warm. He asked my grandmother if she had any light bread baked. She said yes and got it for him. He told her to butter it and lay the butter side down on my mouth and if it melted I was still living. She did this and soon she said, "Yes, he is still alive." He said, "Now go to work and get a little whiskey and butter and beat it together good and drop just two drops in his mouth, and in four hours drop two more." He sat beside me, laid his hands on my breast and about ten o'clock de next day I began to come around. I realized he was there and he asked me if I knew him, which I did.

In "blowing fire," my grandfather simply blew on de burn and de fire and pain was gone. It was a secret charm, handed down from generation to generation. He said only one could be told. He told my Aunt Harriet and she could "blow fire" de same as my grandfather.

I remember one good old doctor in dis part of de country. Old Dr. Stark. He was as good a doctor, de finest we had in those days. He could chew tobacco and spit enough to drown a dog. A lot of de old herb remedies my grandfather used, I can still remember. He used one called "white root." It is a bush dat grows here. In de spring of de year, when its leaves bloom out, in de morning house, when de sun shines on it, it looks just like bright light. It has an awful bitter taste. It was used for mighty near any ailment. He had another herb he used, called "remedy weed." It is a bright-green-looking weed dat grows around springs. It is also used for many ailments. Another one was sarsaparilla root. It grows here, lots of it. He went to de woods and gathered it all hisself getting wild cherry bark, ditney, pennyroyal, and camomile root. Others he gathered and dried; some to make teas and others to put in whiskey.

Dogwood buds, some kind of a medicine used as a laxative. Ginseng was another remedy. I do not know what it was used for, but it was powerful good and one remedy he used was called "spicewood." It was also a healthful drink, like store tea. You gather it in de fall, using de stem or stocky part, break it up and dry it. I used it all de time while I worked on de river, at de tourist camps. It has a fine flavor and it's good for you.

Indian turnip grows by de thousands in de woods here. Great places of it, looks like turnips, grows in big bunches and bright red. Colored folks used to use de Indian turnip in slave times. Dey would take dis and dry it, pulverize it, and tie it in big quantities around dere feet to keep off de trail de bloodhounds. No bloodhound could trail a bit further after smelling it. It was strong like red peppers, burns like everything, and colored folks running away used it all de time.

Grandfather also used "butternut root," some call it white walnut. You take one dose of dis and it will cure de worst case of chills, no matter how bad. Take two tablespoons for a dose. It is as severe as croton oil. By golly, it won't leave a thing in you, clears you out, and one dose does de work. Oh man, but it is bitter.

He used golden seal, a medicine found in places here, very costly, worth seven dollars to eight dollars a pound now. I don't know what he used dem all for, but I do remember him getting dem in their proper seasons, and kept dem always on hand.

For sore throat or quinsy, he had some sort of tea. He used onion tea too. He took an onion, roasted it in its hull in ashes, squeezed out de juice, and added a little sugar, and gave it to de patient. For rheumatism, he used poke root, dried it and put it in whiskey. De only thing dat is good for rheumatics. There were many more remedies, but I can't recall them now.

ROSA STARKE

Interviewed in Winnsboro, South Carolina
Interviewed by W. W. Dixon
Age when interviewed: 83

THEY SAY I was six years old when de war commence poppin' in Charleston. Mammy and Pappy say dat I was born on de Graham place, one of de nineteen plantations of my old master, Nick Peay, in 1854. My pappy was named Bob and my mammy named Salina. They had belonged to old Marse Tom Starke before old Marse Nick bought them. My brothers was named Bob and John. I had a sister named Carrie. They was all older than me.

My marster, Nick Peay, had nineteen places with a overseer and slave quarters on every place. Folks dat knows will tell you, dis day, dat them nineteen plantations, in all, was twenty-seven thousand acres. He had a thousand slaves, more or less, too many to take a census of. Before de numerator get 'round, some more would be born or bought, and de numerator had to be sent 'round by Marse Nick, so old Miss Martha, our mistress, say. Her never could know just how many 'twas. Folks used to come to see her and ask how many they had, and her say it was one of them sums in de 'rithmetic dat a body never could take a slate and pencil and find out de correct answer to.

Her was a Adamson before her marry Old Marster, a grand big buckra. Had a grand manner, no patience with poor white folks. They couldn't come in de front yard; they knowed to pass on by to de lot, hitch up dere hoss, and come knock on de kitchen door and make dere wants and wishes knowed to de butler.

You wants me to tell 'bout what kind of house us niggers live in then? Well, it 'pend on de nigger and what him was doin'. Dere was just two classes to de white folks, buckra slave owners and poor white folks dat didn't own no slaves. Dere was more classes 'mongst de slaves. De first class was de house servants. Dese was de butler, de maids, de nurses, chambermaids, and de cooks. De next class was de carriage drivers and de gardeners, de carpenters, de barber, and de stable men.

Then come de next class—de wheelwright, wagoners, blacksmiths, and slave foremen.

De next class I 'members was de cow men and de niggers dat have care of de dogs. All dese have good houses and never have to work hard or get a beatin'. Then come de cradlers of de wheat, de threshers, and de millers of de corn and de wheat, and de feeders of de cotton gin. De lowest class was de common field niggers. A house nigger might swoop down and mate with a field hand's good lookin' daughter, now and then, for pure love of her, but you never see a house gal lower herself by marryin' and matin' with a common field-hand nigger. Dat offend de white folks, 'specially de young misses, who liked de business of match makin' and matin' of de young slaves.

My young masters was Marse Tom, Marse Nick, and Marse Austin. My young misses was Miss Martha, Miss Mary, and Miss Anne Eliza. I knows Marse Nick Jr. marry a Cunningham of Liberty Hill. Marse Tom marry a Lyles and Marse Austin marry and move to Abbeville, after de war. Old Master die de year before de war, I think, 'cause my mammy and pappy fell in de division to Marse Nick and us leave de Graham place to go to de home place. It was called de Melrose Place. And what a place dat was! 'Twas on a hill, overlookin' de place where de Longtown Presbyterian Church and cemetery is today. Dere was thirty rooms in it and a fish pond on top of it, flower yard stretchin' clean down de hill to de big road, where de big gate, hangin' on big granite pillars, swung open to let de carriages, buggies, and wagons in and up to de house.

Can I tell you some of de things dat was in dat house when de Yankees come? I 'members some things dat would astonish you as it astonished them. They had Marseilles carpets, linen tablecloths, two silver candlesticks in every room, four wine decanters, four nutcrackers, and two coffee pots, all of them silver. Silver casters for pepper, salt, and vinegar bottles. All de plates was china. Ninety-eight silver forks, knives, teaspoons and tablespoons. Four silver ladles, six silver sugar tongs, silver goblets, a silver mustard pot and two silver fruit stands. All de fireplaces had brass firedogs and marble mantelpieces. Dere was four oil paintin's in de hall, each cost, so Marse Nick say, one hundred dollars. One was his ma, one was his pa, one was his Uncle Austin, and de other was of Colonel Lamar.

De smokehouse had four rooms and a cellar. One room, every year, was filled with brown sugar just shoveled in with spades. In winter they would drive up a drove of hogs from each plantation, kill them, scald de hair off them, pack de meat away in salt, and hang up de hams and shoulders around and about de smokehouse. Most of de rum and wine was kept in barrels, in de cellar, but dere was a closet in de house where whiskey and brandy were kept for quick use. All back on de east side of de mansion was de garden and terraces, acres of sweet 'taters, watermelons, and strawberries and two long rows of beehives.

Old Marster die. De appraisers of de 'state come and figure dat his mules, niggers, cows, hogs, and things was worth $200,000. Land and houses I disremember about. They, anyhow, say de property was over a million dollars. They put a price of $1,600 on Mammy and $1,800 on Pappy. I 'member they say I was worth $400. Young Marse Nick tell us dat de personal property of de estate was appraised at $288,168.78.

Ye Yankees come set all de cotton and de gin-house afire; load up all de meat; take some of de sugar and shovel some over de yard; take all de wine, rum, and liquor; gut de house of all de silver and valuables, set it afire, and leave one thousand niggers cold and hungry and our white folks in a misery they never has got over to de third generation of them. Some of them is de poorest white folks in dis state today. I weeps when I sees them so poor, but they is 'spectable yet, thank God.

After de war I stuck to de Peay white folks, till I got married to Will Harrison. I can't say I love him, though he was de father of all my chillen. My pappy, you know, was a half-white man. Maybe dat explain it. Anyhow, when he took de fever I sent for Dr. Gibson, and 'tend him faithful, but he die and I felt more like I was free, when I come back from de funeral, than I did when Marse Abe Lincoln set us free. My brother, Bob, had done gone to Florida.

I next marry, in a half-hearted way, John Pearson, to help take care of me and my three chillen—John, Bob, and Carrie. Him take pneumonia and die, and I never have a speck of heart to marry a colored man since. I just have a mind to wait for de proper sort till I get to heaven, but dese adult teachers destroy dat hope. They read me dat dere is no marryin' in heaven. Well, well, dat'll be a great disappointment to some I knows, both white and black, and de ginger-cake women like me.

MINGO WHITE

Interviewed at Burleson, Alabama
Interviewed by Levi D. Shelby Jr.
Age when interviewed: 85–90

I WAS born in Chester, South Carolina, but I was mostly raised in Alabama. When I was about four or five years old, I was loaded in a wagon with a lot more people in it. Where I was bound I don't know. Whatever become of my mammy and pappy I don't know for a long time. I was told there was a lot of slave speculators in Chester to buy some slaves for some folks in Alabama. I 'members dat I was took up on a stand and a lot of people come round and felt my arms and legs and chest, and ask me a lot of questions. Before we slaves was took to de tradin' post Old Marsa Crawford told us to tell everybody what asked us if we'd ever been sick dat us'd never been sick in our life. Us had to tell 'em all sorts of lies for our marsa or else take a beatin'.

I was just a li'l thing, tooked away from my mammy and pappy, just when I needed 'em most. The only carin' that I had or ever knowed anything about was give to me by a friend of my pappy. His name was John White. My pappy told him to take care of me for him. John was a fiddler and many a night I woke up to find myself 'sleep 'twixt his legs whilst he was playin' for a dance for de white folks. My pappy and mammy was sold from each other, too, de same time as I was sold. I used to wonder if I had any brothers or sisters, as I had always wanted some. A few years later I found out I didn't have none.

I'll never forget de trip from Chester to Burleson. I wouldn't 'member so well, I don't guess, 'ceptin' I had a big old sheep dog named Trailer. He followed right in back of de wagon dat I was in. Us had to cross a wide stream what I took to be a river. When we started cross, old Trailer never stopped followin'. I was watchin' him close so if he gived out I was goin' to try to get him. He didn't give out; he didn't even have to swim. He just walked along and lapped de water like a dog will.

John took me and kept me in de cabin with him. De cabin didn't have no furniture in it like we has nowadays. De bed was one-legged.

140

It was made in de corner of de room, with de leg settin' out in de middle of de floor. A plank was runned 'twixt de logs of de cabin and nailed to de post on de front of de bed. Across de foot another plank was runned into de logs and nailed to de logs. Den some straw or corn shucks was piled on for a mattress. Us used anything what we could get for cover. De table had two legs, de legs set out to de front whilst de back part was nailed to de wall. Us didn't have no stove. There was a great big fireplace where de cookin' was done. Us didn't have to cook, though, lessen us got hungry after supper been served at de house.

I weren't nothin' but a child endurin' slavery, but I had to work de same as any man. I went to de field and hoed cotton, pulled fodder and picked cotton with de rest of de hands. I kept up, too, to keep from gettin' any lashes dat night when us got home. In de winter I went to de woods with de menfolks to help get wood or to get sap from de trees to make turpentine and tar. Iffen us didn't do dat we made charcoal to run de blacksmith shop with.

De white folks was hard on us. Dey would whip us about de least li'l thing. It wouldn'ta been so bad iffen us had a had comforts, but to live like us did was 'nough to make anybody soon as be dead. De white folks told us dat us born to work for 'em and dat us was doin' fine at dat.

De next time dat I saw my mammy I was a great big boy. Dere was a woman on de place what everybody called "Mammy"—Selina White. One day Mammy called me and said, "Mingo, your mammy is comin'." I said, "I thought dat you was my mammy." She said, "No, I ain't your mammy. Your mammy is away from here." I couldn't believe dat I had another mammy and I never thought about it anymore.

One day I was sittin' down at de barn when a wagon come up de lane. I stood round like a child will. When de wagon got to de house, my mammy got out and broke and run to me and throwed her arms round my neck and hug and kiss me. I never even put my arms round her or nothin' of de sort. I just stood dere lookin' at her. She said, "Son, ain't you glad to see your mammy?" I looked at her and walked off. Mammy Selina call me and told me dat I had hurt my mammy's feelin's, and dat dis woman was my mammy.

I went off and studied and I begins to 'member things. I went to Selina and asked her how long it been since I seen my mammy. She told me dat I had been away from her since I was just a li'l chile. I went to my mammy and told her dat I was sorry I done what I did and dat I would like for her to forget and forgive me for de way I act when I first saw her. After I had talked with my real mammy, she told me of how de family had been broke up and dat she hadn't seed my pappy since he was sold.

My mammy never would of seen me no more if de Lord hadn'ta

been in de plan. Tom White's daughter married one of Mr. Crawford's sons. Dey lived in Virginia. Back den it was de custom for women to come home whenever dey husbands died or quit 'em. Mr. Crawford's son died and dat forced her to come home. My mammy had been her maid, so when she got ready to come home she brung my mammy with her.

It was hard back in dem days. Every mornin' before daybreak you had to be up and ready to get to de field. It was de same every day in de year 'cept on Sunday, and den we was gettin' up earlier dan de folks do now on Monday. De drivers was hard, too. Dey could say whatever dey wanted to and you couldn't say nothin' for yourself. Somehow or other us had a instinct dat we was goin' to be free.

In de event when de day's work was done de slaves would be found locked in dere cabins prayin' for de Lord to free dem like he did de chillen of Israel. Iffen dey didn't lock up, de marsa or de driver would of heard 'em and whipped 'em. De slaves had a way of puttin' a wash pot in de door of de cabin to keep de sound in de house.

I 'members once old Ned White was caught prayin'. De drivers took him de next day and carried him to de pegs, what was four stakes drove in de ground. Ned was made to pull off everything but his pants and lay on his stomach between de pegs whilst somebody strapped his legs and arms to de pegs. Den dey whipped him till de blood run from him like he was a hog. Dey made all of de hands come and see it, and dey said us'd get de same thing if us was cotched. Dey don't allow a man to whip a horse like dey whipped us in dem days.

After my mammy come where I was I helped her with her work. Her task was too hard for any one person. She had to serve as maid to Mr. White's daughter, cook for all of de hands, spin and card four cuts of thread a day, and den wash. Dere was one hundred and forty-four threads to de cut. If she didn't get all of dis done she got fifty lashes dat night. Many de night me and her would spin and card so she could get her task de next day. No matter what she had to do de next day she would have to get dem cuts of thread, even on wash day.

Wash day was on Wednesday. My mammy would have to take de clothes about three-quarters of a mile to de branch where de washin' was to be done. She didn't have no washboard like dey have nowadays. She had a paddle what she beat de clothes with. Everybody knowed when wash day was 'cause dey could hear de paddle for about three or four miles. "Pow-pow-pow," dats how it sound. She had to iron de clothes de same day dat she washed and den get dem four cuts of thread.

Lots of times she failed to get 'em and got de fifty lashes. One day when Tom White was whippin' her she said, "Lay it on, Marsa White, 'cause I'm goin' to tell de Yankees when dey come." When Mammy got through spinnin' de cloth she had to dye it. She used sumac berries, indigo, bark from some trees, and dere was some kind of rock what she got red dye from. De clothes wouldn't fade, neither.

De white folks didn't learn us to do nothin' but work. Dey said dat us weren't supposed to know how to read and write. Dere was one feller name E. C. White what learned to read and write endurin' slavery. He had to carry de chillen's books to school for 'em and go back after dem. His young marsa taught him to read and write unbeknownst to his father and de rest of de slaves.

Us didn't have nowhere to go 'cept church and we didn't get no pleasure outen it 'cause we weren't allowed to talk from de time we left home till us got back. If us went to church de drivers went with us. Us didn't have no church 'cept de white folks church.

After old Ned got such a terrible beatin' for prayin' for freedom he slipped off and went to de North to join de Union Army. After he got in de army he wrote to Marsa Tom. In his letter he had dese words: "I am layin' down, Marsa, and gettin' up, Marsa," meaning dat he went to bed when he felt like it and got up when he pleased to. He told Tom White dat iffen he wanted him he was in the army and dat he could come after him.

After old Ned had got to de North, de other hands begin to watch for a chance to slip off. Many a one was cotched and brung back. Dey knowed de penalty what dey would have to pay, and dis cause some of 'em to get desperate. Druther dan to take a beatin' dey would choose to fight it out till dey was able to get away or die before dey would take de beatin'.

Lots of times when de patterollers would get after de slaves dey would have de wors' fight and sometimes de patterollers would get killed. After de War I saw Ned, and he told me de night he left the patterollers runned him for four days. He say de way he hid to keep dem from catchin' him was he went by de woods. De patterollers come in de woods lookin' for him, so he just got a tree on 'em and den followed. Dey figured dat he was headin' for de free states, so dey headed dat way too, and Ned just followed dem far as dey could go. Den he clumb a tree and hid whilst dey turned round and come back. Ned went on without any trouble much. De patterollers used to be bad. Dey would run de folks iffen dey was caught out after eight o'clock in de night, iffen dey didn't have no pass from de marsa.

After de day's work was done there weren't anything for de slaves to do but go to bed. Wednesday night they went to prayer meetin'. We had to be in de bed by nine o'clock. Every night de drivers come 'round to make sure dat we was in de bed. I heerd tell of folks goin' to bed and den gettin' up and goin' to another plantation.

On Saturday de hands worked till noon. Dey had de rest of de time to work dey gardens. Every family had a garden of dere own. On Saturday nights the slaves could frolic for a while. Dey would have parties sometimes and whiskey and home-brew for de servants. On Sundays we didn't do anything but lay round and sleep, 'cause we didn't like to go to church. On Christmas we didn't have to do no work, no more'n feed de stock and do de li'l work round de house. When we got through with dat we had de rest of de day to run round wherever we wanted to go. 'Course, we had to get permission from de marsa.

De owners of slaves used to give corn shuckin' parties, and invite slaves from other plantations. Dey would have plenty of whiskey and other stuff to eat. De slaves would shuck corn and eat and drink. Dey used to give cotton pickin's de same way. All of dis went on at night. Dey had jacklights in de cotton patch for us to see by. De lights was made on a forked stick and moved from place to place whilst we picked. De corn shuckin' was done at de barn, and dey didn't have to have lights so dey could move dem from place to place.

I was a pretty big boy when de War broke out. I 'member seein' de Yankees cross Big Bear Creek bridge one day. All of de soldiers crossed de bridge but one. He stayed on de other side till all de rest had got across, den he got down offen his horse and took a bottle of somethin' and strewed it all over de bridge. Den he lighted a match to it and followed de rest. In a few minutes de Rebel soldiers come to de bridge to cross but it was on fire and dey had to swim across to de other side. I went home and told my mammy dat de Rebels was chasin' de Union soldiers, and dat one of de Unions has poured some water on de bridge and set it afire. She laugh and say: "Son, don't you know dat water don't make a fire? Dat musta been turpentine or oil."

I 'member one day Mr. Tom was havin' a big barbecue for de Rebel soldiers in our yard. Come a big roarin' down de military road, and three men in blue coats rode up to de gate and come on in. Just as soon as de Rebels saw 'em dey all run to de woods. In about five minutes de yard was full of blue coats. Dey et up all de grub what de Rebels had been eatin'. Tom White had to run away to keep de Yankees from gettin' him. Before de Yankees come, de white folks took all dey clothes and hung 'em in de cabins. Dey told de colored folks to tell de Yankees dat de clothes was dere'n. Dey told us to tell 'em how good dey been to us and dat we liked to live with 'em.

De day dat we got news dat we was free, Mr. White called us niggers to the house. He said: "You are all free, just as free as I am. Now go and get yourself somewhere to stick your heads."

Just as soon as he say dat, my mammy hollered out: "Dat's 'nough for a yearlin'." She struck out across de field to Mr. Lee Osborn's to get a place for me and her to stay. He paid us seventy-five cents a day, fifty cents to her and two bits for me. He gave us our dinner along with de wages. After de crop was gathered for that year, me and my mammy cut and hauled wood for Mr. Osborn. Us left Mr. Osborn dat fall and went to Mr. John Rawlins. Us made a sharecrop with him. Us'd pick two rows of cotton and he'd pick two rows. Us'd pull two rows of corn and he'd pull two rows of corn. He furnished us with rations and a place to stay. Us'd sell our cotton and open corn and pay Mr. John Rawlins for feedin' us. Den we moved with Mr. Hugh Nelson and made a share-crop with him. We kept movin' and makin' sharecrops till us saved up 'nough money to rent us a place and make a crop for ourselves.

Us did right well at dis until de Ku Klux got so bad, us had to move back with Mr. Nelson for protection. De mens that took us in was Union men. Dey lived here in the South but dey taken us part in de slave business. De Ku Klux threat to whip Mr. Nelson, 'cause he took up for de niggers. Heap of nights we would hear of de Ku Klux comin' and leave home. Sometimes us was scared not to go and scared to go away from home.

One day I borrowed a gun from Ed Davis to go squirrel huntin'. When I take de gun back I didn't unload it like I always been doin'. Dat night de Ku Klux called on Ed to whip him. When dey told him to open de door, he heard one of 'em say, "Shoot him time he gets de door open." "Well," he says to 'em, "Wait till I can light de lamp." Den he got de gun what I had left loaded, got down on his knees and stuck it through a log and pull de trigger. He hit Newt Dobbs in de stomach and kilt him.

He couldn't stay round Burleson any more, so he come to Mr. Nelson and got 'nough money to get to Pine Bluff, Arkansas. The Ku Klux got bad sure 'nough den and went to killin' niggers and white folks, too.

I married Kizi Drumgoole. Reverend W. C. Northcross perform de ceremony. Dere weren't nobody dere but de witness and me and Kizi. I had three sons, but all of 'em is dead 'ceptin' one and dat's Hugh. He got seven chillens.

ROSE WILLIAMS

Interviewed in Ft. Worth, Texas
Interviewer not identified
Age when interviewed: 90

WHAT STATEMENT I'se make am de facts. I'se not going to Huntsville [Texas State Prison] for nothing. If I'se one day old, I'se 90 for sure. I'se born in Bell County, Texas, and am owned by Master William Black. He owned my mammy and pappy too. I'se too small to have de correct memorandum, but I'se remembers when de war starts, I'se herding sheep and turkeys and tending chickens and such.

Master Black had quite a large plantation, but he owned more niggers dan he needs for work on his place, 'cause he am a nigger trader. He trades, buys, and sells all de time.

Master am awful cruel. He whips de colored folks, works dem hard, and feeds dem poorly. We'uns have for rations de cornmeal, milk, 'lasses, beans, and peas. We'uns had meat twice a week. Dere am not tea or coffee, and such as white flour, we'uns don't know what dat looks like. We'uns have to work in de fields every day from daylight till dark, and on Sunday, we'uns do de washing. Church? Shucks, we'uns don't know what that means.

I'se remembers hearing de folks talking 'bout de war starting when Master Black sold we'uns. Mammy and Pappy am powerful glad to be sold, except dey's worried 'bout being separated, but my folks [wanted] to be sold to some good master. Mammy, Pappy, and I'se put on de block with 'bout ten other niggers.

When we'uns gets to de trading block, dere was a lot of white folks dere dat come to look de slaves over. I'se believe dere was 'bout fifty niggers dere for sale. De white folks am looking dis one and dat one over. Dere am one man dat shows interest in Pappy. Him named Hawkins. He talk to Pappy, and Pappy talks to him and says, "Dem am my woman and childs. Please buy we'uns. I'se portly and strong as de mule." He den says, "A likely looking nigger, but three am more dan I'se wants, I'se guess."

De sale starts and 'twarn't long till Pappy am put on de block. Master Hawkins wins de bid for Pappy, and when Mammy am put on de block, he also wins de bid for her. Den dere am two or three other niggers sold before my time comes. Den Master Black calls we'uns to de block. De auction man says, "How much am I'se offered for dis portly strong young wench? She never been abused and will make a good breeder."

I'se wants to hear Master Hawkins bid, but him says nothing. Two other men am bidding against each other. I'se sure have de worryment. Dere am tears coming down my cheeks 'cause I'se being sold to some party dat would cause separation from my mammy. One of de bidders bid $500, and de auction man am asking, "Do I'se hear more? She am going at $500."

Den someone says, "$525." No one bid higher, and de auction man says, "She am going for $525. She am going for $525. She am sold for $525 to Master Hawkins." Am I'se glad and excited? Why, I'se quivering all over.

Master Hawkins took we'uns to his place, and it am a nice plantation. Lots better dan Master Black's. Dere am 'bout fifty working niggers on de place. De first thing de master does when we'uns gets home am give we'uns rations and a cabin. White man, you'se believe dis nigger when I'se says dem rations was a feast for we'uns. Dere was plenty of meat, some tea, and a little coffee. I'se never taste white flour before, nor de coffee. Mammy made some biscuits and fix some coffee. Well, de biscuits was yum, yum to me, but de coffee I'se don't like.

De quarters for de colored folks am 'bout like it am on Master Black's place. Dere am twelve cabins and all made from logs with just a table, benches, bunks for sleeping, and a fireplace for cooking and de heat. Dere am no floor, just de ground.

Master Hawkins never forces de niggers to work on Saturday afternoon or on a Sunday, except when dey am rushed with de work, and he never overworks his colored folks. Dere am as much difference 'twixt Master Hawkins and Master Black in de way of treatment as dere is 'twixt de Lord and de devil. Master Hawkins allows his niggers to have reasonable parties, allows dem passes for to go places, and allows dem to go fishing sometimes, but we'uns never am tooken to church, and dere am no books on de place for learning, so dere am no education for de niggers.

Dere am one thing dat Master Hawkins does to me dat I'se cannot shut from my mind. I'se know dat he don't do it for meanness, but I'se will always hold it 'gainst him. What he done am forced me to live with nigger Rufus 'gainst my wants.

After I'se am at Master Hawkins' place 'bout a year, de master comes to me one day and says, "You'se going to live with Rufus in dat cabin over dere." Him points out de one and tells me to fix it for living. I'se 'bout seventeen years old den and, course, had no learning. I'se just ignorant child. I'se thought dat him means for me to separate from my folks and tend to de cabin for Rufus and some other niggers. Well, dat am de start of pestigation for me.

I'se took charge of de cabin after my work am done and fix supper, den I'se goes here and dere and talks to other folks till I'se ready for sleep, and den I'se goes and fix my bunk. After I'se in de bunk, dat nigger comes and crawls in de bunk with me before I'se knows what he am a-doing.

"What you'se mean? You'se fool nigger, a-getting in my bunk," I'se says to him.

"Hush you'se mouth! Dis am my bunk too," he says.

"You'se tetched in de head. Get out!" I'se told him, and I'se put my feet 'gainst him, give him a shove, and out he goes on de floor before he knows what I'se a-doing. Dat nigger jumps up, and am he mad. He looks like a wild boar. He starts for de bunk where I'se is, and I'se jump quick for de poker. It am 'bout three feet long and when he comes at me, I'se let him have it over his head. Did dat nigger stop in his tracks? I'se says he did. He looks at me steadily for a minute. You'se could tell him am thinkin' hard 'bout me. Den he goes and sits on de bench and says, "Jus' wait. You'se think it am smart, but you'se am foolish in de head. Dey's going to learn you something."

"Hush you'se big mouth and stay 'way from dis nigger, dat's all I'se wants," I'se says to him, and just sits and holds dat poker in my hand, and he just sits a-looking like de bull. Dere we'uns sits and sits for 'bout an hour. Den he goes out and I'se bar de door.

De next day, I'se go to de missy and tell her what Rufus wants to do. De missy says dey am de master's wishes. She says, "You'se am a portly girl, and Rufus am a portly man. De master wants you'uns for to bring forth portly children."

I'se thinking 'bout what de missy says but says to myself, "I'se not going to live with him." Dat night when Rufus comes in de cabin, I'se grabs de poker and sits on de bench and says to him, "Keep away from me, nigger, 'fore I'se bust you'se brains out and stomp on dem." He says nothing and leaves de cabin.

De next day de master calls me to him and tells me, "Woman, I'se pay big money for you'se, and I'se done dat for de cause I'se wants you'se to raise me chilluns. I'se put you'se to live with Rufus for dat purpose. Now, if you'se don't want to be whipped at de stake, you'se do what I'se want."

I'se think 'bout de master buying me off de block and save me from being separated from my folks and 'bout being whipped at de stake.

Dere it am. What am I'se to do? So I'se decides to do as de master wishes and so I'se yield.

When we'uns am given de freedom, Master Hawkins tells all us colored folks dat we'uns could stay and work for wages or sharecrop de land. Some of de folks stay and some of de folks left. My folks and me stayed. We'uns worked de land on shares for three years, den moved to other land near de master's place. I'se stayed with my folks till dey's died, and den I'se went to work for other folks.

If my memorandum am correct, it am thirty years ago dat I'se come to Fort Worth. Here I'se work for white folks as de cook till I'se go blind. Dat am 'bout ten years ago.

Married? Never! No sir! One experience am 'nough for dis nigger. After what I'se do for de master, I'se never want any truck with any man. De Lord forgive dis colored woman, but he have to 'scuse me and look for some other persons for to replenish de earth. Anyway, it's too late now. I'se done lived my life.

For de last ten years, my white and colored folks friends tend to me having food and a place to sleep. I'se thankful for dat. In a little while, dis nigger will go to Jordan, and den we'uns shall have rest and peace.